Studies in Modern History

VIETNAM

STUDIES IN MODERN HISTORY

VIETNAM

HUGH HIGGINS

Second Edition

HEINEMANN EDUCATIONAL BOOKS

LONDON AND EXETER

Cover photograph: A family escaping from the fighting in Saigon, May, 1968. (UPI)

STUDIES IN MODERN HISTORY

The Cold War, Hugh Higgins
Cold War to Détente, Colin Bown and Peter J. Mooney
China 1949–76, Colin Brown
America since 1920, Daniel Snowman
The Soviet Superpower, Peter J. Mooney

Heinemann Educational Books Ltd
22 Bedford Square, London WC1B 3HH

Heinemann Educational Books Inc.
4 Front Street, Exeter, NH 03833, USA

LONDON EDINBURGH MELBOURNE AUCKLAND
HONG KONG SINGAPORE KUALA LUMPUR
NEW DELHI IBADAN NAIROBI JOHANNESBURG
EXETER (NH) KINGSTON PORT OF SPAIN

Library of Congress Data

(Studies in Modern History)
Bibliography: P.
Includes Index.
1. Vietnamese conflict, 1961–1975 -- United States
2. Vietnam -- History -- 1945–1975
3. Vietnam -- History -- 1975
R4 United States History - 1945- I. Title
II. Series: Studies in Modern History (Heinemann Educational Books)

DS558.H5 1982 959.704′33′73 82–11787
ISBN 0–435–31399–1

Printed in Great Britain
by Fletcher and Son Ltd, Norwich

CONTENTS

PREFACE TO THE SECOND EDITION

In 1973 a group of journalists working in the British press, radio and television examined the treatment by those media of the Vietnam War. They concluded that there had been and still was an overwhelming bias in favour of the official American line. One of my reasons for writing the first edition of this book was to give readers a chance to see the recent history of Vietnam from a standpoint other than that of Western governments. I attempted to give due weight to the work of, for example, Chomsky, Halberstam and Fitzgerald.

Despite the continuing efforts of Chomsky and others, misrepresentation of Vietnam's history has persisted to the present time. Since 1975 critics of the new government in Vietnam have accused it of seeking to dominate the whole of Indochina, thereby dragging the entire region within the Soviet sphere of influence. Pham Van Dong and his colleagues have thus been cast in the roles both of 'hegemonists' and puppets of Moscow. The contradiction inherent in that assessment stems, I believe, from an inability, or a reluctance, to understand what in fact were the objectives of the Vietnamese leaders between 1975 and 1980. In the last three chapters of this new edition I have tried to present what is, I trust, a more realistic, albeit brief, account of that period. Inevitably, this can be only an interim statement: later writers will have access to sources not now available. Of the sources I have been able to consult, I wish to mention in particular the informative and objective reports by Nayan Chanda, the principal Vietnam correspondent of the *Far Eastern Economic Review*.

Hugh Higgins
January 1982

ACKNOWLEDGEMENTS

The author and publishers would like to thank the following for permission to reproduce photographs and cartoons:

Camera Press: figs. 1, 2, 5, 6, 7, 8, 9, 11, 12, 15, 21.   Etablissment Cinématographique des Armées: fig. 3. Paul Popper: fig. 4. Associated Press: fig. 10. Romano Cagnoni: fig. 13. New Statesman: fig. 14. The Observer: fig. 16. Eupra Press: fig. 17. Abbas/Rex Features: fig. 18. Keystone Press: fig. 19. Miami News: fig. 20.

One

THE IMPACT OF FRENCH RULE: OPPOSITION TO THE FRENCH

In the twentieth century proponents of empire have commonly underestimated the power of nationalism. Their misjudgment is nowhere more evident than in the recent history of Vietnam. Political leaders both in France and the United States have, through contempt for their nationalist opponents, made crucial decisions about Vietnam without the slightest understanding of the actual situation. They viewed the country in terms of its relevance to French or American interests, seemingly unaware that Vietnam could not be understood without reference to its own history and culture. It was, admittedly, a land remote from their experience. One historian has indeed claimed that 'culturally Vietnam is quite beyond the normal range of occidental comprehension'.[1]

The hackneyed image of the inscrutable orient was the product of an imperialist mentality. The fact was that empire-builders from the West made little effort to comprehend the societies they conquered. Their task was not to understand the 'natives' but to transform them. Non-white societies were considered to be under-developed both materially and culturally; only contact with the West could overcome their backwardness. Such ethnocentric convictions of white superiority have proved exceedingly tenacious. They were exemplified by President Lyndon Johnson when, shortly after launching his attack on North Vietnam, he explained how American technology would help to release the peoples of Southeast Asia from impoverishment. 'I want,' he declared, 'to leave the footprints of America there. We're going to turn the Mekong into a Tennessee Valley.'[2]

Johnson and his advisers failed to understand that basic changes in the Vietnamese way of life could be achieved only by forward-looking people from Vietnam itself. Such people, being fully conscious of the obscurantism of traditional Vietnamese society, had no illusions about the size of the problem. They themselves rejected ancestor-worship and the Confucian notion that an emperor, the Son of Heaven, should be obeyed as the mediator between heaven and the people. At the same time they appreciated that the culture based on Confucian principles had, for a thousand years, helped to propagate and maintain a sense of national identity among the Vietnamese people. The disintegration of that culture during the latter part of the nineteenth century had set them adrift. The challenge of the twentieth century was to put Vietnam on a new course, to create a new society which would have the cohesion but not the social injustice of the old.

Before recording the struggles of the reformers it is necessary to look back briefly to the end of the old society. Its destruction was the work of the French, whose incursion into Vietnam formed part of a take-over of most of Asia by Western imperialists and whose superior technology gave them control of all Indochina within a generation. Between 1858 and 1859 they occupied the area around Saigon. From 1861 they encroached on Cochinchina (the southern part of Vietnam) which they controlled by 1885. During 1883–4 they established their protectorate over the northern and central parts of the country. In the course of conquering Cochinchina they also incorporated the neighbouring kingdom of Cambodia into their empire as a protectorate. Towards the end of the century, in 1893, they compelled the Siamese government to cede the territory of Laos. Occupation of Siam itself was prevented only by imperial rivalry between France and Britain. The British had annexed Upper Burma in 1886 and were concerned about French activities in that area, since they wished to avoid a common frontier between British India and French Indochina. Siam was, therefore, allowed to remain as an independent buffer state.

In Vietnam colonization proceeded rapidly and thoroughly, its several aspects reflecting the aims of the various factions in French colonialism. Missionary groups of the powerful Roman Catholic Church wished to spread the gospel among the heathen. Merchants and financiers sought profit from the exploitation of natural resources. Ambitious politicians and administrators aspired to 'leave the footprints' of France in a backward land. To achieve their objectives the French assumed control of Vietnam's political system and refashioned its commercial and economic structure.

The political system was radically changed, despite the façade of continuity provided by the emperor, who retained some of the trappings of the Son of Heaven. He was, in fact, powerless and the mandarins, who previously had ruled on his behalf, now worked for his colonial masters. The Confucian system itself was undermined with the encouragement of Catholic missionaries, the putative leaders of 'la mission civilisatrice'. Since time immemorial the Vietnamese had been socialized in the belief that their ancestors were the source of their lives and their civilization. Worship of their ancestors was bound up with their feelings towards the land itself which, as the resting place of their fore-bears, was held sacred. The people 'flowed over the land like water, maintaining and fructifying it for the generations to come'.[3] Thus, in attacking the 'heathen' practice of ancestor-worship, mission-aries threatened to disrupt the entire life-style of the vast majority of the Vietnamese people.

The economic changes were also far-reaching. A predomin-antly agricultural society, providing a bare subsistence for the mass of peasants, did not offer sufficient scope for foreign capitalists who, therefore, attempted an economic transformation. The 1860s saw an enormous increase in the rice paddies of Cochin-china and the growth of a large export trade in rice. (By the 1930s Cochinchina was the world's third largest rice exporter, after Burma and Siam.) Industry also expanded. At the turn of the century there was increasing investment in the mining of coal and other minerals: the production of coal, tin and zinc accelerated rapidly in the period after the First World War. Later – in the 1930s – the development of extensive plantations resulted in a substan-tial export trade in rubber.[4]

Such changes were intended to create in Indochina an economic enterprise exploitable by the mother country. A few figures help to illustrate how far they succeeded. In 1938, two years before their Indochinese empire was overwhelmed by the Japanese, the French provided 95 per cent of the European capital invested in business enterprises and all the capital invested in government securities. They also dominated Indochinese trade: in 1938 53 per cent of Indochina's exports went to France. Between 1931 and 1938 Indochina's imports from France averaged 57 per cent of its total imports.[5]

Despite the economic impact of French rule the economy of Vietnam remained predominantly agrarian. Even in 1940 the peasants still constituted between 85 and 90 per cent of the population. Changes were, however, taking place, particularly in the system of land ownership. They were especially marked in Cochinchina where the extension of rice cultivation and rubber plantations put large estates in the hands of a small landed class with control of 80 per cent of the rice-fields, where some 200,000 families were employed in sharecropping. Sharecroppers commonly paid the landlord 40 per cent of the crop, in addition to furnishing various gifts and services – a practice reminiscent of some feudal system. Furthermore, tenants were obliged to pay exorbitant interest on their landlord's capital and for any credit advanced by him. Peasants who had a small holding of their own were also forced to pay huge sums in interest – up to 120 per cent per annum – to moneylenders. All peasants suffered additionally from high taxation imposed by the government, which also operated a monopoly on the purchase and distribution of alcohol, opium and salt, thus removing from the villages their secondary means of livelihood.[6]

Village communities were weakened in other ways: when, for instance, village notables were made to relinquish their authority to officials trained by the French. Deprived of their natural leaders, those communities became more vulnerable to outside pressures. Much of their land fell into the hands of mandarins who had chosen to help both the French and themselves. As communal life was disrupted and population increases accentuated the scarcity of land, the villages lost more of their members to new urban centres and industrial enterprises such as rubber plantations. Although villages continued to be the focus of life in the countryside, they were less able to hold their communities together and they had lost much of their former autonomy.

French rule created a new societal structure in Vietnam. Those who benefited from the colonial dispensation included the large landowners and a small, mainly foreign, upper class of capitalists. There also emerged, as a result of economic developments, a small middle class. At the bottom of the pyramid were those exploited by the first groups: the landless tenants and an emergent working class composed of miners, plantation workers, public works employees and industrial labourers. Somewhat apart from the other groups was a comparatively large intelligentsia – a disillusioned élite, ready to provide recruits for factions opposed to the colonial regime.[7]

It is worth noting here that the nature of opposition to French rule altered significantly over the years. The French had imposed a new kind of domination whose overthrow required new forms of national awareness and different modes of political action.[8] What began as a struggle to reinstate the old Confucian system was transformed into a demand for drastic changes within Vietnamese society. Conflict developed not only between the nationalists and the French but also among the nationalists themselves. Traditionalists opposed those who sought to restructure society. Within the ranks of the reformers there was a division between advocates of change by constitutional means and others who worked for a revolution.

During the first decades of the French regime there was a series of revolts led by those mandarins who, having refused to collaborate with the conquerors, were determined to restore the old system. The most notable was the so-called Scholars' Revolt of 1885, an attempt to seize power in the name of the young emperor Ham Nghi.[9] Inspired by the moral authority of the scholars and mandarins who led the revolt, the peasants rallied to the cause. Their struggle persisted for three years, impressing even the French by its tenacity. Finally, in 1888, Ham Nghi was captured, after many of his followers had been killed in battle or succumbed to disease. The brutality of the colonial troops in putting down the revolt helped to provoke more mandarin-led-uprisings in the course of the next ten years. Such localized efforts to turn back the clock were suppressed with increasing severity and by 1900 the traditionalists had virtually shot their bolt. Every defeat they suffered was a reminder that the old monarchy was incapable of providing effective resistance to the foreigners, who enjoyed modern weapons and superior organization. How could a dynasty which had lost the country its independence and then had failed to restore it, claim that it had the mandate of heaven? Many concluded that it could not and new resistance movements emerged with aims other than the re-establishment of the traditional monarchy.

One man who epitomized the new nationalism was Phan Boi Chau.[10] He argued that, in order to overthrow the French, it was necessary to learn from them. Vietnamese society must, he felt, be modernized before it could regain its independence. In 1905 he visited Japan, whose Meiji emperors had, as a result of westernization, been able to create a formidable military power. During the Russo–Japanese war Japan had imposed a humiliating defeat on the Russian empire which undermined the myth of white supremacy and inspired nationalist movements throughout Asia.[11] Chau believed that Vietnam should follow the Japanese example. Accordingly he founded a Reform Association to win freedom under the leadership of a reformed monarchy. In 1908 it supported a popular protest in Central Vietnam against high taxation and corvée labour.[12] It was the first anti-French demonstration by peasants demanding redress of specific grievances. However, neither Chau nor his lieutenants fully appreciated at that stage the potential of peasant movements. The French easily put down the rebellion and arrested most of its leaders. Chau himself fled to Japan.

Some years later, in 1911, a revolution in China overthrew the Manchu dynasty and Chau, who had previously been impressed by its prime mover, Sun Yat-sen, made his way to Canton. Dazzled by the success of Sun's Kuomintang (Nationalist) party, Chau abandoned his schemes for a reformed and reforming monarchy and established, in 1912, the Viet-Nam Phuc-Quoc Hoi (Vietnamese Independence Association) with the aim of creating a democratic republic in Vietnam. From his base at Canton Chau was, for more than a decade, 'the most determined and radical Vietnamese agitator and the most effective political educator, the man the French regarded as the most dangerous nationalist revolutionary . . .'[13] He was the instigator of several uprisings and numerous insurrectionary incidents until his career as a revolutionary ended in 1925 with his arrest by the French.

Although Phan Boi Chau had, for a quarter of a century, caused the French a great deal of trouble, they were in 1925 still firmly ensconced in Vietnam and apparently able to cope with all attempts to remove them. Chau, for all his zeal, had serious weaknesses. His talent as an agitator was flawed by an inability to expound effectively the purpose of his revolutionary activity. The modernization of Vietnam was an unhelpfully vague goal and Chau neglected to provide a practical programme of specific political and economic demands. Nor did he make productive contact with the mass of Vietnamese, the peasants. He concentrated his effort on the élite and tended to count on outside help rather than on decisive action from the Vietnamese themselves.

1. Ai Quoc (Ho Chi Minh) reads the declaration of independence of the provisional government, September 1945.

Shortly before Chau was arrested a Vietnamese nationalist of a different stamp arrived in Canton. Nguyen Ai Quoc had been sent by the Communist International to join a mission, led by Michael Borodin, whose task was to aid Sun Yat-sen in organizing the Kuomintang. Ai Quoc's main concern, however, was not to strengthen the nationalist movement in China, but to create an effective revolutionary force in Vietnam. For nearly half a century he was to play a major role in Vietnamese politics. In the period between the wars he was the inspirer of a new brand of revolutionaries. After the Second World War he became the dominant figure in his own country and achieved world-wide fame under the name he adopted in 1942 – Ho Chi Minh.[14]

Ho was born with the name Nguyen Sinh Cung in 1890 in Nghe An, a province noted for the rebelliousness of its inhabitants. From his father and his environment he acquired a hatred of French imperialism and a strong sense of patriotism. In 1911 he left Vietnam as a cabin boy and spent two years at sea. During that time he visited a number of countries and became increasingly concerned with politics – in particular with the plight of his native land. In 1917 he made his way to Paris where he built up contacts with the numerous Vietnamese who, in the course of the First World War, had been sent to France. He became their spokesman and recruited their services for the struggle to gain recognition and betterment for Vietnam. (It was at this time that he adopted the name Ai Quoc, the patriot.) In 1919 he drew up a programme for the emancipation of his country which included requests for permanent representation in the French parliament, freedom of the press, an amnesty for political prisoners and equality of legal rights between French and Vietnamese. The programme was forwarded to the secretariat of the Paris Peace Conference, then attempting to settle the affairs of the world after the end of the war, but was not discussed. Clemenceau Lloyd George and Wilson, the men who dominated the conference, were selective in their anti-imperialism. While they enthusiastically dismembered the empires of Germany and Austro–Hungary, they preserved and even extended their own. Communism rather than imperialism was their enemy.

It was to the communists that Ai Quoc turned for support. At the Eighteenth Congress of the French Socialist Party, held in December 1920, he inveighed against the 'abhorrent crimes' committed by imperialists against his native land and voted in favour of joining the Third International. Founded in Moscow in 1919, the Third (Communist) International was dedicated to the expansion of communism as an international movement. Its moving spirit was Lenin, whose writings had turned Ai Quoc into a dedicated revolutionary.

Many years later he explained that at first he had respected Lenin 'purely because he was a great patriot who had set his countrymen free'.[15] Subsequently he was deeply impressed by Lenin's theses on the problem of nationalities and the colonial peoples. 'My joy was so great,' he commented, 'that at times I was reduced to tears. Alone in my room, I would cry out as though standing before a great crowd: "My beloved, downtrodden, luckless compatriots! This is what we need, this is our road to freedom!"'[16] In the first place it was patriotism, not communism, that led him to believe in Lenin and the Third International. Eventually, after studying Marxism–Leninism and involving himself in practical work, he became convinced that only communism was 'capable of bringing freedom to the oppressed and to working people all over the world'.[17]

In 1923 Ai Quoc was sent to Moscow as the French Communist Party delegate to the Peasant International. He remained to study communism and, in 1924, to attend the Fifth Congress of the Comintern. Thereafter, as already noted, he joined Borodin in Canton where he began to organize an Indochinese communist movement. In February 1930 he persuaded three competing communist groups to unite to form the Vietnamese Communist Party which, to emphasize its international character, renamed itself in October the Indochinese Communist Party (Dong Duong Cong San Dong).[18] The newly united party was soon put to the test by a major rising of the peasants in Nghe An province.

Open rebellion occurred in northern Annam during the summer of 1930, when famine was added to the other miseries of the people. Consequently the communist party succeeded in activating not only the peasants but also factory workers in the provinces of Nghe An and Ha Tinh. The main force was provided by the peasantry, six thousand of whom staged a hunger march on 12 September to the town of Vinh. The colonial administration was totally disrupted and replaced by local councils called xo-viets. These Vietnamese soviets managed to survive for several months, instituting a programme of reforms which allowed the communists to claim that the revolution had been put into effect. Their success was however short-lived; early in 1931 the French assembled enough troops to take the offensive. The repression that followed demonstrated the ferocity of an imperial power when it felt threatened. It is estimated that 10,000 Vietnamese were killed and 50,000 deported. Buttinger has commented: 'People were killed not in the heat of battle – there were no battles – but rather they were chased, hunted down, and murdered by a soldiery drunk on blood.'[19]

The scale of the Nghe An rebellion contrasted significantly with an uprising organized by the Vietnamese Nationalist Party (Vietnam Quoc Dan Dang). Founded three years previously it modelled itself on the Kuomintang in China, seeking to replace French dominion with a republican government on the lines of the regime led by Chiang Kai-shek. In February its leaders staged a mutiny of the Vietnamese garrison troops at Yen-Bay in Tonkin which was intended to initiate a chain reaction of incidents culminating in a full-scale revolution. Owing to faulty organization and poor security the French had no difficulty in suppressing the uprising at its inception. The Nationalist leaders were executed and the party itself never recovered. Henceforth revolutionary movements in Tonkin were dominated by the communists.[20]

Despite the setbacks caused by the white terror of 1931, Nguyen Ai Quoc was greatly encouraged by the events of the previous year. The unified communist movement in Indochina had gained a psychological victory with the Nghe An revolution. While the terrorist methods of the Nationalist Party had proved wholly ineffective, the setting up of the soviets in Annam and their capacity to organize a mass movement had convinced many peasants that a successful revolution was possible. The French, it appeared, could be ousted if only the rural population were mobilized on the side of an armed independence movement.

Even so, nearly a quarter of a century elapsed before the French were finally forced from Vietnam, their withdrawal being precipitated by events outwith the control of the Vietnamese nationalists. In 1939 the French declared war on Nazi Germany. Within a year they were forced to capitulate and were powerless to prevent Hitler's ally, Japan, from assuming control of their empire in Indochina. It was only during the Japanese occupation that an effective nationalist movement at last emerged.

The nature of that movement had been determined by the lessons learned in the period between the two world wars. During those years it became evident that the gradualist approach of those who sought independence by constitutional means could not succeed. The constitutionalists were an urban élite who failed to find any significant following in the countryside.[21] While they were prepared to work within the system created by the colonial power, the support of the rural masses was being won by those who appreciated that the system could not be manipulated; that it must be destroyed. It was evident that the French had no intention of sharing power in any foreseeable future. Such Vietnamese participation as did exist, for example in Cochinchina, was spurious: it stopped well short of the point at which decisions were made.

In fact the French ruled by coercion, not through consultation. The situation therefore demanded a conspiratorial rather than a constitutional opposition. To survive in a police-state it was essential to create the kind of underground network at which the communists excelled. Another aspect of French rule which the communists turned to their own advantage was the economic policy. Its blatant exploitation of the Vietnamese economy provided a most telling confirmation of the Leninist critique of imperialism. As one historian has observed, the subordination of Vietnam to French economic interests was for young Vietnamese 'a classic example of the imperialist state's treatment of a colony. It was Viet-Nam's fate, or less dramatically its historical experience, that Marxist ideals should have appealed to men who proved themselves to be the best organized and the best able to lead.'[22]

The Vietnamese masses meanwhile knew nothing of Marx. Their hatred of the French derived from the misery of their lives and a deeply rooted national consciousness. Foreign dogma had little appeal to men who revered above all their land and their ancestors. The leaders of the communist party realized however that without the backing of the peasants there would be no socialist revolution. Marx himself had dismissed the peasants as mere beasts of burden and Stalin, the voice of world communism, considered that the vanguard of the revolution must be drawn from the urban workers. Nguyen Ai Quoc, more a man of action than an armchair theorist,[23] was convinced that, regardless of orthodox Marxist opinion, the peasants could make excellent recruits to the cause of revolution. The Nghe An experience had shown what could be achieved. The next stage was to raise the revolutionary consciousness of peasants throughout Vietnam. Ten years after Nghe An the disruption caused by the Second World War gave Ai Quoc his chance.

Two

THE WAR AGAINST THE FRENCH
1946–54

The fall of France in 1940 was followed by the establishment of the pro-Nazi Vichy government, a collaborationist regime with Marshal Pétain at its head. Supporters of Pétain also assumed control of the French administration in Indochina, where they co-operated fully with the Japanese in their campaigns against the Vietnamese nationalists. As a result of the Nazi–Soviet Pact[1] the communists in Vietnam were at first under orders not to oppose the Japanese. In 1941 they were extricated from that invidious position when Hitler invaded the Soviet Union. Thereafter both Germany and Japan were officially recognized as imperialist aggressors. Even before Stalin's enforced volte-face Nguyen Ai Quoc had founded, in May 1941, the League for Vietnamese Independence (Vietnam Doc Lap Dong Minh), soon to become famous as the Vietminh.

Although it was set up at a meeting of the central committee of the Indochinese Communist Party, the Vietminh was intended to attract support not only from communists but from all shades of nationalist opinion. In June 1941 it made the following appeal; 'Rich people, soldiers, workers, peasants, intellectuals, employees, traders, youth and women who warmly love your country! At the present time national liberation is the most important problem. Let us unite together!'[2] The genuineness of that appeal has been a matter of some debate. Certain historians have argued that the Vietminh was essentially a nationalist movement with its emphasis on 'the country's history, the Flag, Vietnamese culture . . .'[3] Others have contended that it was merely a cover for the communists; that while it posed as a union of patriots, in fact it was 'hiding its real ideological nature until such time as independence had been won'.[4] The issue has often been put in a more personal way. Was Ho Chi Minh in essence a nationalist whose communism was more a means than an end? Alternatively, was he a communist above all, who found it convenient to masquerade as a nationalist? Such questions are best considered after we have examined the history of the Vietminh. At this point we might note that Ho considered such a dichotomy pointless. He saw himself as both a nationalist and a communist, the one role complementing the other.[5]

His problem, after the founding of the Vietminh, was not, however, to scrutinize his own motives but to gain the maximum support for his new organization. China, Vietnam's northern neighbour, was the nearest source of aid. Since 1936 there had been in China an alliance, albeit uneasy, between the communists and the Kuomintang in order to defeat the Japanese, who had launched a full-scale invasion of the country in 1937. In order to make contact with both groups Ho crossed into China in July 1942 and was promptly arrested by the Kuomintang. He spent the next fifteen months in shackles, hustled from jail to jail, covered with scabies and half-starved. Eventually he was released, when his captors realized that he might be of some use to them. At that stage of the Second World War Chiang Kai-shek, the head of the Kuomintang, had the firm support of the allied leaders and was expected to remain as the dominant figure in China when the Japanese were defeated. It was even proposed that he might assume control of the northern part of Vietnam. With that prospect in mind, the Kuomintang were anxious to win over local support and in October 1942 established the Vietnam Revolutionary Alliance (Dong Min Hoi). They were soon forced to realize that without the support of the Vietminh the alliance would make little headway. Accordingly, Ho Chi Minh was released and made leader of the Dong Min Hoi! The nationalist cause in Vietnam was thus reinforced by the very people who thought they were undermining it. Its outstanding leader gained not only his freedom but also the co-operation of the Kuomintang, who clearly underestimated his talents as a dissembler.

During the next two years the Vietminh provided the main resistance to the Japanese and gained the sympathy and admiration of American military intelligence officers who fought at their side. One of the US leaders in the field advised his superiors: 'Forget the communist bogy. VML [the Vietminh League] is not communist, stands for freedom and reforms from French harshness. If French go part way with them they might work with French.'[6] Later reports described Ho as a 'brilliant and capable man' and commented that his troops 'made up . . . in spirit what they lacked in training'.[7] With American support Ho established a strategic base-area in the Cao-Bang province of Vietnam and was fully prepared to take advantage of two crucial events in the final stage of the war in Asia.

The first was the *coup d'état* in Vietnam by the Japanese on 9 March 1945. Within twenty-four hours the Japanese army disarmed and imprisoned French military units in Indochina. At the same time all French officials were dismissed and many interned. Now that the war was clearly going against them the Japanese no longer trusted their former collaborators. In supplanting them they put an end, for the time being, to French influence in Vietnam. Before the coup the Vietminh had two enemies to contend with; after it only the Japanese stood between them and independence, but not for long. On 6 August 1945 the Japanese city of Hiroshima was totally destroyed by one atomic bomb. Three days later a second bomb devastated Nagasaki and the Japanese government quickly sued for peace. On 13 August the Vietminh formed a National Liberation Committee; within a week they controlled Hanoi and became in effect a provisional government. Bao Dai, the puppet emperor of Vietnam under the Japanese, abdicated and on 2 September in Hanoi, Ho Chi Minh, his beard blowing about and his voice heavy with emotion, proclaimed his country's independence.[8]

The Declaration of Independence of the Democratic Republic of Vietnam began, ironically enough in the light of later events, with a quotation from the American Declaration of Independence of 1776: 'All men are created equal. They are endowed by their Creator with certain inalienable rights, among these are Life, Liberty and the pursuit of Happiness.' It went on to describe how the French had denied such rights to the Vietnamese: '. . . they have deprived our people of every democratic liberty . . . They have enforced inhuman laws . . . They have built more prisons than schools . . . they have drowned our uprisings in rivers of blood . . . They have fleeced us to the backbone, impoverished our people and devastated our land . . . They have hampered the prospering of our national bourgeoisie; they have mercilessly exploited our workers.' Having condemned past misdeeds, it then anticipated a better future: '. . . we, members of the Provincial Government, representing the whole Vietnamese people, declare that from now on we break off all relations of a colonial character with France . . . The whole Vietnamese people, animated by a common purpose, are determined to fight to the bitter end against any attempt by the French colonialists to reconquer their country.'[9]

Their declaration of independence was made at the end of a war ostensibly on behalf of democracy and the Vietnamese hoped for powerful support against any French move to reimpose colonial rule. They were convinced, they said, that the Allied nations would not refuse to acknowledge the independence of a people who had fought with them against the fascists. Vietnam had the right to be free and independent and, they affirmed, was so already. The blunt statement that Vietnam had already gained its independence was, in a sense, true. As we have seen, Ho Chi Minh had established a government in the north. At the same time a People's Committee was set up in Saigon under Tran Van Giau, the communist leader of the southern Vietminh. The French historian Devillers has recorded that 'ten days after the Japanese capitulation, the Vietminh controlled the entire territory of Vietnam'.[10] Meanwhile France itself was in a desperate plight. The ravages of war had turned the whole country upside down and the prospect of the French regaining control of their former empire in Indochina seemed remote.

Given that Vietnam was *de facto* an ex-colony, its government might have been organized under a trusteeship, as had been suggested by the American President, Roosevelt. He was highly critical of the French colonial record and believed that the people of Indochina deserved something better. His prescription was a trusteeship exercised by the great powers who would supervise the progressive development of the Vietnamese towards self-government. At the Yalta Conference of February 1945 the proposal had a mixed reception. According to Roosevelt, while the Soviets and the Chinese were agreeable, the British opposed it, fearing that it might break up their empire: 'if the Indo–Chinese were to work together and eventually get their independence the Burmese might do the same thing.'[11]

Roosevelt had no chance to modify the British attitude since he died in April 1945. At the next meeting of the great powers, held at Potsdam in July and August, America was represented by a new president, Truman, who was concerned less about French colonialism than about Soviet imperialism. In his opinion, liberating the Vietnamese from the French was a secondary issue. The big question was how to contain the Soviet Union. He accepted the need for some changes in Vietnam, but only under the auspices of the French. There was to be no trusteeship in Indochina except under the French government, which would be asked 'at some appropriate time' to say what its intentions were regarding basic liberties and some movement towards self-determination.[12]

Truman's policy shift pleased not only the French but also the British. They, no less than the French, had been humiliated by the Japanese in the early years of the war in the Pacific. Asian peoples had seen them driven from Hong Kong, Singapore and Burma. Even India, the jewel of the British Empire, had been menaced by the Japanese. The restoration of that empire to its former power was one of Churchill's main objectives in 1945. It could not be restored without holding in check the nationalist forces which had been encouraged by the defeats sustained by the white colonial powers. The British had long experience of dealing with nationalism and knew how contagious it was. Like Roosevelt, they realized that if Indochina broke away from France it would be so much harder to contain other Asian peoples within the British empire. Whatever Churchill's view of the French, he was bound to favour them against the Vietnamese.

To everyone's amazement, Churchill himself was not present at the second session of the Potsdam Conference. His unexpected electoral defeat resulted in a Labour government under Attlee who, unlike Churchill, had considerable sympathy for the nationalist movement in India. Indeed, within three years of his coming to power, both India and Burma gained their independence. However, at the time of the Potsdam Conference he had been in office only for a few weeks. It was hardly likely that in so short a time he would re-orientate British policy in Southeast Asia. The conference in fact confirmed that, pending a final settlement, Indochina should be divided at the sixteenth parallel. China was to control the northern part while the south came under the jurisdiction of Mountbatten, the British commander in the Pacific. His instructions were to take over the Japanese headquarters and disarm and repatriate their troops. In addition, he was to release and transport home allied prisoners-of-war. He was to occupy no more territory than was necessary to carry out his orders and was to withdraw his troops as soon as possible. A similar brief was given to the Chinese.

The Potsdam decision seriously weakened the position of the nationalists in Vietnam. For a time, admittedly brief, the Vietminh had been the only effective force in the country. The dreams of the revolutionaries seemed to have come true. Their enemies were defeated, their country united and their right to rule themselves was about to be confirmed by all the allies. However, far from recognizing their independence, the allies had superseded the authority of the Provisional Government by partitioning the country and occupying it with the armies of two of the major powers. We consider first the impact of the British in the south.

At first the nationalists expected co-operation from the British and arranged a friendly reception for General Gracey when he arrived in Saigon on 13 September 1945. The Vietminh decorated the route from the airport to the city with British, American and Vietminh flags and pro-allied slogans, one of which read 'Welcome to the Allies, to the British and the Americans, but we have no room for the French.'[13] Very quickly, however, the British outlived their welcome. Although the Vietminh had assumed control of Saigon and, given the circumstances, were running a fairly efficient administration, Gracey refused to have any dealings with them. He had no doubt that the French were entitled to restore their empire and that it was, therefore, pointless to recognize the nationalists.

Fearful that their influence was being eroded the Vietminh organized boycotts and demonstrations against the British. Gracey retaliated by closing their newspapers and enforcing martial law. On 23 September he permitted a group of French troops and civilians, whom he had armed the previous day, to seize the Vietminh headquarters. Most of them had been prisoners of the Vietminh since the surrender of Japan and were determined to take revenge for their former humiliations, which they did with excessive brutality. Even the most moderate Vietnamese were alienated by the shootings and beatings that followed: people who had once been willing to negotiate terms, 'after being gun-whipped and thrown into jail emerged as bitter opponents of French rule'.[14]

As usual, violence begat violence. On 25 September European and Eurasian civilians were massacred in the Cité Hérodia, a suburb of Saigon; estimates of the dead vary from 150 to 300. The massacre was probably the work of the Binh Xuyen, thugs from the Saigon underworld. Nevertheless, the Vietminh were held responsible and Gracey decided to crush them. In the war that followed he relied heavily on the Japanese troops in the area, thus reducing the casualties of his own British and Indian soldiers. MacArthur, the American commander in the Pacific, declared: 'If there is anything that makes my blood boil, it is to see our allies in Indo-China . . . deploying Japanese troops to reconquer these little people we promised to liberate. It is the most ignoble kind of betrayal.'[15] In January 1946 Nehru, one of the leaders of the nationalist movement in India, told the *New York Times*: 'We have watched British intervention . . . with growing anger, shame and helplessness, that Indian troops should be used for doing Britain's dirty work against our friends who are fighting the same fight as we.'[16]

Nehru's protest was made when the issue was apparently settled. By early 1946 Gracey's forces had destroyed, at least temporarily, nationalist resistance in the south of Vietnam. Their victory was the object of some criticism even in Britain. Laski, an influential figure in the Labour Party, believed that the intervention in Indochina made 'the British claim to have been engaged in a war for democracy and freedom seem a hollow mockery all over South-East Asia'.[17] Outlining the official attitude, Bevin, the Foreign Secretary, explained that the government did not wish to be involved in the affairs of non-British territories. Therefore it had expedited the movement of French troops to Saigon to enable them to relieve the British.[18] From the outset it had assumed that the French should be re-established in Indochina. In the light of subsequent developments we might feel that the British policy was disastrously mistaken. It would, however, have been a remarkably bold move to stand in the way of the French. What, we might consider, would have been the reaction in France, and in the USA, if the British had favoured the Vietminh? What grounds were there for believing that the nationalists in the south were capable of sustaining a stable administration? Was it realistic to expect a new and inexperienced government to effect a reversal of policy which would have caused repercussions throughout the whole of Asia, including a major upheaval in India?

Discounting such considerations, Rosie has argued that British actions set the scene for a prolonged confrontation. He claims that the British force destroyed a genuinely popular revolution and put down the risings which followed. Had it not done so the French would probably have been obliged to come to terms with the nationalists. If, he asks, 'the French had been forced to assume a moderate position in 1945, would the world have seen the protracted Franco–Vietminh war of 1946–54 and the American–Vietnamese war of today?'[19]

There is no doubt that the re-imposition of French control in the south strengthened their standing throughout the country. Even so, under Ho Chi Minh, the Vietminh in the north had begun a programme of action which gained them considerable public confidence. Ho was confident enough himself to organize general elections which were held in January 1946, not only in northern and central Indochina but also secretly in numerous parts of the French zone in the south. The results, which gave the Vietminh a clear majority in the assembly, were, according to one authority, 'probably fairly indicative of the state of public opinion at that time'.[20] The new government won further support through the effectiveness of its campaign to produce more food when its people were threatened with starvation, a common occurrence in Southeast Asia. In the words of the American historian, Ellen Hammer: 'when the Spring of 1946 came, the people did not starve. Conditions were still not good, but the VietMinh had succeeded in doing what the French had not always been able to do: they had saved the country from famine by the unaided efforts of their citizens.'[21]

Although his government had proved the viability of self-determination, and while some of his supporters demanded a total break with the colonial past, Ho Chi Minh was prepared to negotiate with the French. He appreciated the possible advantages of co-operation with France and was also apprehensive about the influence of the Chinese, who, under the terms of Potsdam, had an army of between 150,000 and 185,000 men in occupation of northern Indochina. For twenty years the Kuomintang had been in conflict with their indigenous communists; it was hardly likely that they would look favourably on a communist-dominated administration in Hanoi. Bearing in mind the clash of ideologies and the long memory of Chinese intervention in Vietnam, Ho's apprehension seemed to be well founded. 'It is better,' he is reported as saying, 'to sniff France's dung for a while than eat China's all our lives.'[22] In fact the Chinese Nationalists did not aim to stay permanently in Vietnam. Their main concern was to strengthen their hold in China itself against the encroachments of the communists. Thus, in February 1946, they recognized French sovereignty over Indochina. At the same time the French surrendered their territorial and economic privileges in China. The Franco–Chinese settlement exerted pressure on Ho Chi Minh to come to terms with the French, whose 'rights' in Vietnam had been endorsed by both occupying powers.

On 6 March 1946 Ho's government agreed to give the French a friendly reception when they relieved the Chinese troops. In return the French recognized the republic of Vietnam as a free state, with a government, a parliament, and an army: a state which formed part of the Indochinese Federation and the French Union. This supposed settlement in fact settled nothing, being 'little more than an armistice that provided a transient illusion of agreement where no agreement actually existed'.[23] Giap, later to become the outstanding Vietminh general, compared it to the Brest–Litovsk treaty the Bolsheviks had made with the German High Command in 1918. It was a humiliation to be endured in order to give the Vietminh time to create an effective fighting force and should be repudiated as soon as possible.[24] The powerful colonial lobby in France looked on the agreement with equal distaste. For them also it was a means of buying time while they consolidated their forces in the south. Both Ho and the more moderate leaders in France came under attack from their own sides.

Ho's visit to France in June 1946 did little to improve matters. Even before he reached Paris, d'Argenlieu[25] had set up a so-called 'autonomous republic' in Cochinchina: an obvious device for dividing Vietnam while the French manoeuvred to regain control of the whole country for themselves. With the conflict between the extreme nationalists and the neo-colonialists becoming increasingly bitter there was a desperate need for some moderator; but none appeared. It was only one year since the end of the Second World War and the great powers had more urgent problems to deal with. They were, in any case, divided themselves. The alliance created by the struggle against Germany and Japan disintegrated as the Cold War ensued. Furthermore, the major issue in the Far East was not the fate of Vietnam but the conflict between the Kuomintang and the communists in China.

In September 1946 Ho Chi Minh made a further agreement with the French which did little more than recapitulate the ineffectual settlement of the previous March. But the time for compromise was running out. France was passing through a constitutional crisis: disgusted with the old Third Republic, the French were seeking an alternative form of government. While they were preoccupied with founding the Fourth Republic, the conduct of affairs in Vietnam was left to the most uncompromising enemies of the nationalist movement. The Vietminh responded to the intransigence of the *colons* with acts of terrorism. Towards the end of November the French retaliated by shelling the port of Haiphong from the cruiser *Suffren*. Six thousand Vietnamese were killed and with them died the remote possibility of a peaceful solution. Within a month Ho was exhorting his countrymen to rise against the French: 'Let him who has a rifle use his rifle, let him who has a sword use his sword! And let those who have no sword take up pick-axes and sticks.'[26]

The *colons*, seriously underestimating the strength of an enemy whom they dismissed contemptuously as 'les jaunes', expected an easy victory over the Vietminh. After a year of fighting the French Minister of War felt able to announce that 'there was no longer any military problem in Indo-China'.[27] At the same time the *Journal de Saigon* claimed that Ho Chi Minh represented 'nothing at all'.[28] As the war dragged on, the French were forced to admit that the Vietminh did have considerable support and that the military problem was persisting. Accordingly they tried to weaken the Vietminh by establishing another Vietnamese regime. On 14 June 1949, Bao Dai was proclaimed head of the 'new' state of Vietnam. This French manoeuvre to solve an intractable military problem with a political device failed. Bao Dai's only hope of attracting people away from the Vietminh was to make himself credible as an independent leader. It was obvious, however, that he owed his position to the French. His government was made up of nonentities – no one of national reputation would serve under him.

On the other hand, their campaign against the French had toughened the morale of the Vietminh and enhanced the authority of Ho Chi Minh. Suffering economic and financial strain, the French were embroiled in a war against a resourceful enemy, while their potential allies simply looked on. Although the American government was apprehensive about the Vietminh's communist affiliations, it was not prepared to intervene. Even after Bao Dai was offered as a non-communist alternative to Ho the State Department declared: 'We cannot at this time irretrievably commit the US to support of a native government which . . . might become virtually a puppet government separated from the people and existing only by the presence of French military forces.'[29]

The situation changed dramatically when, in October 1949, the Chinese Communists finally ousted the Nationalists and set up their own government. In December their troops reached the northern border of Vietnam. On the thirtieth of that month President Truman approved a National Security Council study on Asia which recommended that the USA provide 'political, economic and military assistance and advice' to areas threatened by communist aggression. It suggested that 'particular attention should be given to the problem of French Indochina'. In February 1950 the French made a request for military aid which was sympathetically received by Acheson, the US Secretary of State. He warned Truman that if America failed to support the 'legal governments in Indochina' it would 'face the extension of Communism over the remainder of the continental area of South-east Asia and possibly westward'.[30] The American government announced in May that it would make the French an initial grant of $10 million.[31] Objectively the conflict in Vietnam may have seemed much as before: communist-led nationalists trying to unseat the French. Viewed from Washington, however, the war had become part of the free world's struggle against international communism.

It is important to consider why the US became at this point 'directly involved in the developing tragedy in Vietnam'. What persuaded them that a localized colonial war fitted into the pattern of a world-wide communist conspiracy? Early in 1950 the communist government in China had given diplomatic recognition to the Democratic Republic of Vietnam; on 31 January the Soviet Union followed suit. That recognition, said Acheson, 'should remove any illusions as to the "nationalist" character of Ho Chi Minh's aims and reveals Ho in his true colours as the mortal enemy of native independence in Indochina'.[32] Acheson's statement betrays the Cold War psychosis that was then affecting American policy.

There can be little doubt that Ho Chi Minh wanted, above all, to achieve independence for Vietnam; it was the cause to which he had devoted his whole life. What he sought from his fellow-communists in Moscow and Peking was recognition, not domination. The Vietminh had made their own revolution in 1945 and since then had fought alone against the French. There was no reason for making themselves pawns of Mao or Stalin. Nor was there any evidence that they had done so. There was ample evidence, however, that the American leaders had been badly shaken by the defection, as they saw it, of China to the communist camp. What impelled them to help the French was not so much the absurd assumption that Ho Chi Minh had become a Soviet puppet, but rather the stark fact that Mao Tse-tung controlled China. Disturbed by the implications of that fact, the US over-reacted and saw China as a greater menace that it was. Having discarded the illusion that the Chinese Nationalists could hold China, they then deluded themselves that the Communist Chinese were poised to seize the whole of South-east Asia. This led to the conviction that the Vietminh were not genuine nationalists but merely a communist fifth-column. It became imperative therefore to support the French anti-communist crusade. The outbreak of war in Korea, in June 1950, made them even more determined to maintain French control of Indochina.

2. General Vo Nguyen Giap with a young anti-aircraft gunner.

However, despite American financial and other support, the French made little headway against the Vietminh. To explain their failure we must look beyond the purely military aspect of the war. Not everyone saw it as an anti-communist crusade. Many Frenchmen still felt that it was a colonial war which was becoming more difficult to justify as nationalist movements elsewhere were being recognized by former colonial powers. The British, for example had retired from India and Burma. The Dutch had been obliged to concede self-rule to their East Indian possessions. While a swift victory in Indochina might have been recognized as an accomplished fact, a protracted and inconclusive struggle was becoming unacceptable. General Giap's estimation of the war was proving to be correct. 'The enemy', he had predicted, 'will pass slowly from the offensive to the defensive. The blitzkreig will transform itself into a war of long duration. Thus, the enemy will be caught in a dilemma – he has to drag out the war in order to win it and does not possess, on the other hand, the psychological and political means to fight a long drawn out war.'[33]

By 1954 such means were virtually exhausted. Although the USA was already bearing nearly 80 per cent of the cost of the war effort, the French needed even more help to avoid defeat. Having sustained some 90,000 casualties during more than seven years of guerrilla warfare, they determined, in the spring of 1954, on a major confrontation with the Vietminh at Dienbienphu.[34] French military leaders imagined that Giap's primitive supply system would be inadequate to provide the resources for a pitched battle, and expected that his irregulars would be overwhelmed by their own professional troops. It was a disastrous miscalculation. The Vietminh did in fact concentrate enough men and materials, including artillery, to take on the French. Dienbienphu was besieged and its garrison decimated by artillery bombardment and human-wave attacks. At the end of March its airfield was destroyed. Thereafter the garrison's only hope was the breakthrough of a relieving force from Hanoi or Laos, 'a hopeless concept in view of the terrain and distances involved', or the destruction of the Vietminh by massive aerial bombardment.[35] At the beginning of April the French requested immediate intervention by American carrier-based aircraft to save the day.

While Dulles, the Secretary of State, and Radford, Chairman of the Joint Chiefs of Staff, strongly favoured intervening, other

3. French soldiers dug in at Dienbienphu.

US service chiefs were more cautious. It was finally decided that America should not move on its own. Dulles had to inform the French that, while the American government was 'doing everything possible . . . to prepare [a] public, Congressional and Constitutional basis for united action', such action was not possible without 'active British Commonwealth participation'.[36] At Geneva, where an international conference on Korea and Indochina opened in April, Dulles canvassed British support. Eden, the British Foreign Secretary, promised to examine the situation afresh if the conference failed, but declined to take part in armed intervention at that juncture. While understanding American reluctance to act unilaterally, Bidault, the Foreign Minister of France, warned his allies that it was in fact too late to form a coalition since the fate of Indochina would be settled very shortly at Dienbienphu.[37]

The Vietminh did indeed overwhelm the remnants of the garrison on 7 May, a victory whose timing gave it the maximum political effect: the Indochina phase of the Geneva Conference began on the following day.

Three

THE FAILURE OF THE GENEVA SETTLEMENT: THE RULE OF NGO DINH DIEM IN THE SOUTH

The Geneva Conference was convened because the Vietminh could not be defeated. Had there been any hope of a military victory, the French would have rejected negotiation. The fact that they had been forced to the conference table shocked not only the French but also their friends in Britain and America. While French armies floundered in Vietnam, the British had suppressed a communist movement in Malaya and the Americans had supervised the defeat of a left-wing revolution in the Philippines.[1] After the collapse of the Geneva settlement, counter-insurgency techniques which had succeeded in those countries were employed in Vietnam, where they failed. Before we consider the terms of the settlement it is worth examining why Vietnam proved to be a special case.

The insurgency in Malaya (1948–54) was instigated by the Malayan Communist Party which, despite its name, was almost wholly Chinese in composition. (About 50 per cent of the population was Malay, the rest being mainly Indian and Chinese.) By the early 1950s some 8,000 armed communists were pitted against a much larger force of regular soldiers, police and village 'Home Guards'. Although few in number the communists posed a serious threat to the existing system and extraordinary methods were required to defeat them. Nevertheless they suffered from two fundamental weaknesses. First, they began as a minority faction and failed to attract support from ethnically different groups in the population. Second, while their terrorist campaign was being waged the colonial power promised self-government in Malaya.

The Hukbalahap revolution (1946–54) in the Philippines was the continuation of a movement which had originated before the Second World War with the aim of attacking landlordism in central Luzon. During the war the Huks were the backbone of resistance to the Japanese and contributed substantially to their final defeat. Totally disillusioned thereafter with the corruption and reactionary ineptitude of the ruling clique, the Huks attempted to overthrow the government. For a time their guerrilla tactics proved quite effective against a poorly led and badly equipped Philippine army but from the end of 1950 their strength ebbed. There were two major reasons for their failure. In the first place, their influence was localized. While conditions in their heartland, Luzon, were particularly favourable for an anti-establishment revolution, they were not replicated elsewhere, although there were ample grounds for social unrest throughout the Philippines. Secondly, the Huks were attacking a government which was, at least on the surface, independent. (In practice the US played a dominant role in the political and economic life of the islands.)

Turning to Vietnam, we can see that the Vietminh did not suffer from the basic weaknesses of the Chinese in Malaya and the Hukbalahap. Unlike the Malayan communists the Vietminh were ethnically the same as the rest of the population and were able to attract mass support. (It is worth noting the difference also between the colonial policies of the British and the French.) Similar contrasts can be made about the situation in the Philippines: for example, unlike the Huks, the influence of the Vietminh was not localized. During the long course of the struggle in Vietnam various experts were to suggest that anti-insurgency lessons learned in Malaya and the Philippines could be applied in Indochina. However, despite certain similarities, there were significant differences among the three areas of revolt. Perhaps the most fundamental was that, in contrast with the Vietminh, 'neither the Huks nor Malaya's Chinese insurgents could convincingly claim the nationalist mantle'.[2]

The question of Vietnamese nationalism was of major concern to the members of the Geneva Conference and the demarcation of national boundaries one of their principal tasks. Both the US and the South Vietnamese governments consistently misrepresented the decisions taken about boundaries. In particular they claimed that Vietnam had been divided into two states. The truth was that the settlement provided for a temporary division of the country to allow passions to cool. Thereafter, the temporary dividing line was to disappear, leaving one Vietnamese state which would include territories both north and south of the seventeenth parallel. Thus Article 1 of the Agreement on the Cessation of Hostilities

stipulated a 'provisional military demarcation line'. The forces of the People's Army of Vietnam were to be regrouped north of the line and the forces of the French Union to the south. An interval, after the regrouping had taken place, would allow some of the scars of a long war to heal. Only then would the future of the whole country be decided. The Final Declaration, paragraph seven, stated: 'In order to ensure that sufficient progress in the restoration of peace has been made, and that all the necessary conditions obtain for free expression of the national will, general elections shall be held in July 1956, under the supervision of an international commission . . .'[3]

The balance of forces in Vietnam at the time of the settlement indicated that the Vietminh would, in due course, control the whole country. Their main strength lay in the north, where they had done most of their fighting. With the departure of the French, there was no rival to their authority and they were able to begin the task of post-war reconstruction immediately. Even in the south there were numerous Vietminh supporters. (At Geneva the Vietminh had renounced 20 per cent of the territory it controlled and more than a million and a half inhabitants.[4]) Furthermore the south had, in the course of the war, become a political jungle in which warlords, bandits, secret societies and religious sects were rending each other. Contemporary French observers considered that there was little prospect of an effective administration emerging from such chaos.[5]

Ho Chi Minh urged those unfortunate enough to live in the south to endure the present. As a life-long advocate of a united, independent Vietnam he did not like even the 'temporary' split. However, he recognized the need to settle for less than an immediate total victory. He warned, for example, against those who 'see the French yet do not see the Americans'.[6] He himself saw the Americans clearly enough and understood that the very magnitude of the Vietminh victory at Dienbienphu, together with the political confusion in the south, would make them all the more determined to intervene in Vietnam. On 15 July 1954 he told the Central Committee of the Lao Dong (Communist) Party: 'At this moment American imperialism, the principal enemy of the peoples of the world, is becoming the direct principal enemy of the peoples of Indo-China; that is why all our actions must be aimed at this one enemy.'[7]

4. The Geneva Conference 1954: Bulganin, Eisenhower, Faure and Eden.

For their part the Americans appreciated that their main enemy in Indochina was Ho himself. President Eisenhower recognized in his memoirs the extent of Ho's appeal to his compatriots. 'I have never', he stated, 'talked or corresponded with a person knowledgable in Indochinese affairs who did not agree that had elections been held as of the time of the fighting, possibly 80 per cent of the population would have voted for the communist Ho Chi Minh . . .'[8] Clearly the US could not lightly accept a situation where a communist leader had such enormous popular support. To maintain American interests in Southeast Asia it was necessary to act against the Vietminh and to ensure that, in so far as the Geneva settlement might favour them, it would not be enforced. Eden, chairman of the final session of the Geneva Conference, had expressed the hope that it might have helped to strengthen the forces working for peace. The American leaders, however, felt that more important than peace was the containment of communism; and in their view a Vietminh victory was simply a communist triumph. Thus, while Eden was making his optimistic valedictory a small group of Americans was already preparing to carry on the struggle against the Vietminh.

Under the leadership of Colonel Edward Lansdale – one of the US advisers who helped the Philippine authorities to put down the Huks – the Saigon Military Mission entered Vietnam on 1 June 1954. It was a self-styled 'cold war combat team' whose objective was to carry out para-military operations against the 'enemy' and to wage political-psychological warfare. While the French and the Vietminh made great efforts to observe the terms of the settlement, Lansdale's team, in his words, 'pitched in' to fulfil its 'work load'. That load included the following: an abortive attempt to destroy the presses of the largest printing establishment in North Vietnam; the successful contamination of the oil supply of the Hanoi bus company to cause the wreckage of bus engines; writing detailed notes about potential targets and even the compilation of a bogus almanac predicting disaster for the Vietminh and success for the south.[9]

The military mission was an early earnest of US intentions to undermine the Geneva accords. At the beginning of August 1954 the National Security Council declared that the settlement 'completed a major forward stride of Communism which might lead to the loss of Southeast Asia'.[10] The use of the word 'loss' reveals a good deal about US foreign policy. In 1950 Senator Joseph McCarthy launched his career with the charge that the Truman Administration had connived at the loss of China to the Reds. Such terminology was characteristic of cold war attitudes which posited a division of the world into 'communist' and 'free'. Nations which ceased to be fully committed to the 'free world', that is the system of alliances dominated by the USA, were lost to the other side. Truman had given wide currency to the notion of a dichotomy in his doctrine, enunciated in 1947. 'At the present moment in world history', he declared, 'nearly every nation must choose between alternative ways of life.' It was a choice between democracy and totalitarianism; the role of the United States being to help those who opted for democracy and to defend them against 'armed minorities' and 'outside pressures'. As may become clear, US policy makers tended to interpret the term 'democracy' rather loosely. Indeed, according to Walter Lippmann, the Truman Doctrine led America into 'subsidizing the reactionary forces of the world'.[11]

Eisenhower followed the Truman line when on 20 August 1954 he approved a National Security Council paper on American policy in the Far East. The US thereby undertook to provide military, economic and political support for the anti-communist regime of Ngo Dinh Diem in South Vietnam. In a formal sense the support was conditional: Eisenhower's offer made the proviso that Diem's government should give assurances about 'the standards of performance it would be able to maintain'.[12] In practice, however, American prestige had been committed to 'defending' South Vietnam and it would be hard for any president to end that commitment. The Americans found that they had to tolerate very low 'standards of performance' from Diem and his successors.

During his first year in office Diem's position was rather precarious. Conditions in South Vietnam were so chaotic that in December 1954 General Lawton Collins, Eisenhower's personal representative, recommended that US plans for assisting Southeast Asia be re-evaluated.[13] The situation became even more fraught for Diem when, in the spring of 1955, the Hoa Hao and Cao Dai sects united with the Binh Xuyen gangsters, who controlled Saigon's police, in order to overthrow him. Collins persuaded Dulles that Diem must go. Diem, however, had the support of Lansdale who, through judicious bribery, managed to buy off some of the opposition. Diem then confronted the Binh Xuyen with regular army units and the power of the sects was broken. Henceforth Diem had full American backing and emerged as the strong man who would create a viable anti-communist state in South Vietnam.

Ngo Dinh Diem was a member of an aristocratic and, as we shall see, numerous family. As a devout Roman Catholic he was a thoroughgoing opponent of communism. His religion and his politics made him popular with such influential men as Cardinal Spellman and Senator John F. Kennedy when he visited the United States in 1950. The connections made during that visit strengthened his bid for the leadership of South Vietnam four years later.[14] Once he consolidated his position in 1955 he enjoyed, for the next eight years the confidence of his American allies.

Without their support he would not have remained in power in 1955 and 1956. Only the threat of US intervention prevented the Vietminh overrunning the south after Diem had refused even to

5. President Ngo Dinh Diem.

discuss the elections which, according to the Geneva settlement, were to be held in 1956. The Final Declaration stated that consultations about elections should be held between representatives of the two zones from 29 July 1955 onwards. Four days before that date Diem rejected any proposal from the Vietminh unless they could prove that they would 'put the superior interests of the national community above those of Communism'.[15] Instead of dicussing elections, the authorities in South Vietnam encouraged demonstrations against communist 'misdeeds' and against the Geneva agreement. In Saigon the police arrested more than 100 men and women for demonstrating in favour of consultations about elections. Elsewhere in the south people were imprisoned for explaining the provisions of the settlement to their friends.[16]

The Vietminh, on the other hand, reaffirmed the agreements, pointing out that the division of the country was intended to be temporary and demanding that elections be arranged. They warned the south on 6 June 1955 that whoever tried to partition Vietnam was the enemy of the Vietnamese people and would surely be defeated.[17] However they had no hope against the Americans who were determined to maintain a non-communist regime in the south. The NSC policy statement of August 1954 had made clear the lengths to which they were prepared to go. Not only would the president use his executive power to authorize overt and covert support; he would also, if necessary, get Congressional authority to use military forces locally or against any outside pressures, including Communist China. Such action would be taken to defeat 'local Communist subversion or rebellion *not constituting armed attack*'.[18] [italics added] Thus the US leaders were ready to seize upon any move made by the Vietminh as a pretext for intervening in Vietnam.

Lacking any countervailing support from China or the Soviet Union, the Vietminh could only look on while Diem perpetuated the partition of Vietnam. Not only did he block elections: he also sealed the border between the two halves of the country. After rejecting a North Vietnamese request for the opening of trade relations he also prevented any postal exchange between the two regions, thus keeping totally apart thousands of families whose members had been divided by the vagaries of war.[19] Regardless of the desire of most Vietnamese for a united country Diem consolidated his own power. In October 1955 he arranged a referendum to determine the form of government in the south. Ostensibly there was a choice between a monarchy under the playboy Bao Dai and a republic led by Diem. In practice the result was foregone. Diem received what even American observers described as a 'too resounding' 98.2 per cent of the vote.[20] Although somewhat embarrassed by such blatant gerrymandering, the US government was pleased with its protege. Aid poured in: by 1956 it totalled $250 million per annum, most of it earmarked for 'security'. The Pentagon history cites the example of a twenty-mile highway, built at the request of the US Military Assistance Advisory Group, which was allocated more money than the total sum provided for labour, community development, social welfare, health and education between 1954 and 1961.[21]

Such an order of priorities did no harm to Diem's reputation among the Americans. During the first years of his rule he was hailed as a hero in the USA – the 'tough miracle man' who, having halted 'the red tide of Communism in Asia', was creating a new nation in South Vietnam. In 1961 Vice-President Johnson described him as 'the Winston Churchill of Asia'. Also in 1961 a State Department paper claimed that between 1956 and 1960 there had been 'something close to an economic miracle in South Vietnam'. The production of foodstuffs, textiles and other consumer goods had risen dramatically. Diem's government, it claimed, had successfully settled 900,000 refugees from the north; had helped 300,000 tenant farmers with an agrarian reform programme and had increased loans to peasant families five-fold between 1957 and 1959. A rural health scheme had provided dispensaries for half the villages and hamlets. Between 1956 and 1960 the elementary school population had risen from 400,000 to 1,500,000. The State Department concluded that it was 'a record of progress over a few brief years equalled by few young countries'.[22]

Despite the fulsome public acclaim for Diem, some Americans had considerable private reservations about his government. An intelligence report of May 1959 noted that a façade of representative institutions concealed an essentially authoritarian regime. Intelligence experts also cast doubt on Diem's agrarian reforms. Far from redistributing land to the poor peasants, the government had returned to the landlords those holdings that had been given to the peasants by the Vietminh. Thus 15 per cent of the people still owned 75 per cent of the land. Furthermore, a report compiled at the beginning of 1960 by the US Embassy in Saigon claimed that Diem's coercive measures had made the population apathetic and resentful; there was no rapport between the government and the people.[23]

American criticisms at this stage were largely confined to confidential documents and reports. Even in 1961, however, some doubts were expressed openly about the economic miracle. In an article sub-titled 'Lavish aid limited progress', an American economist argued that South Vietnam was excessively reliant on the large US aid programme which had been directed to military spending and importing consumer goods. Instead of stimulating economic growth it had encouraged the Saigon regime to be a permanent mendicant. The withdrawal of aid would leave the army unpaid and the civilian population unfed. In the light of those facts, the economist's verdict was that the US government had built a 'castle in sand'.[24]

That judgment assumed, of course, that the aim of the aid programme was to encourage the South Vietnamese to create a viable economy. If, however, its prime purpose was to benefit the US economy it might be considered highly successful. According to one view, the aid programme enabled US corporations to establish bridgeheads from which they assumed complete control over the economy of South Vietnam.[25]

Whatever its true objective the programme in fact left the mass of the Vietnamese as poor as they were before it began. While 90 per cent of the population were peasants only 3 per cent of American aid went on rural projects.[26] Disgruntled peasants swelled the mounting criticism of the regime. Despite repression, the non-communist opposition was becoming, by 1960, increasingly vehement. At the beginning of November an influential journal warned that the people were being badgered into a revolution. Since the most elementary rights were denied, it was necessary to replace the government by forceful means. The right-of-centre nationalists felt that they must act quickly: there was a race against the clock between the Vietminh and themselves.[27]

Diem's dictatorship was creating the very revolution that for years he had worked to prevent. In 1955 he initiated an 'anti-communist' denunciation campaign which resulted in the detention of between 50,000 and 100,000 people. The camps held not only communists but also the leaders of religious sects and the smaller political parties, together with journalists and trade-unionists who were 'unco-operative'.[28] The rounding up of opponents became more frequent and brutal during 1958 when the methods of the security forces antagonized many villagers. 'A certain sequence of events became almost classical: denunciation, encirclement of villages, searches and raids, arrests of suspects, plunderings, interrogations enlivened sometimes by torture (even of innocent people), deportation, and "regrouping" of populations suspected of intelligence with the rebels . . .'[29] The Self-Defence Corps and the Civil Guard who carried out such operations were usually ill-trained, poorly equipped and badly led. Their brutality and misconduct turned many peasants into revolutionaries.[30]

Persecuted nationalists and harassed peasants were outside critics. There was also growing disillusion about Diem within the ranks of the government itself. One of its causes was the outrageous nepotism practised by the Ngo family.

Diem's brother, Ngo Dinh Nhu, was his political adviser, with an authority rivalling that of the president himself. The Can Lao Party, created by Nhu in 1954 and responsible to him, wielded immense power, partly because all government officials assumed that it was very powerful. Nhu was also the author of the regime's official philosophy, Personalism – 'an incomprehensible hodge-podge having something to do with state power, the dignity of the Person . . . and the virtues of humility, renunciation and sacrifice.'[31] Such virtues were conspicuously lacking in Nhu's wife, known to US journalists as 'the Dragon Lady'. She was a powerful person in her own right: the First Lady of South Vietnam (Diem being a bachelor), a member of the National Assembly and a leading figure in the Women's Solidarity League, a para-military organization for the defence of the ruling clique. (Her father was Ambassador in Washington.) In family discussions she spurred on her husband and brothers-in-law to impose the authoritarian rule she felt the country required.

Ngo Dinh Can, another brother of the president, needed no prompting. Throughout the period of the regime he was dictator of the whole of central Vietnam. Another important member of the family was Archbishop Ngo Dinh Thuc, the eldest brother and one of Diem's closest advisers. The youngest brother, Ngo Dinh Luyen, who had little influence, served as Ambassador to Britain.

The Ngo family was adept at turning its power to its own material advantage: corruption and nepotism went hand in hand. Nhu financed himself and his various subversive organizations by means of extortion, illicit opium trading and currency swindles. Ngo Dinh Can treated central Vietnam as a personal business enterprise, controlling the local shipping and cinnamon trade and keeping officials under his thumb by graft and extortion. Madame Nhu also acquired a personal fortune in goods which could easily be converted into assets in Europe. She was said to have owned, *inter alia*, a large theatre on the Champs Elysées.[32] Ngo Dinh Diem, himself concerned with power rather than feathering his own nest, turned a blind eye on the depredations of his rapacious relations.

The historical significance of such corruption was that, for the Ngo family, the maintenance of its own power and prestige took precedence over all else. The fate of South Vietnam was, by comparison, of secondary importance. Diem trusted no one outside his family and adopted a policy of 'divide and rule' to prevent strangers usurping his authority. So determined was he to ensure that no rivals could emerge, that he even sabotaged military operations and replaced officers who were competent with those who were corruptible. He was, as someone suggested, not so much running a government as running an opposition within it.[33]

On 11 November 1960 a number of army officers, led by Colonel Nguyen Chahn Thi, attempted a *coup d'état* in which paratroops besieged the presidential palace and occupied a number of key points in Saigon. The rebels promised to establish 'true democracy and liberty' in South Vietnam and to continue the fight against communism. Freedom of the press, assembly and opinion were to be proclaimed. Within 48 hours the revolt was over. The regime was saved by Diem's divide and rule tactics: in the atmosphere they created the army officers did not trust each other. They feared that the leader of a successful coup might oust the rest of them as well as the Ngos. Thus on 12 November loyal units came to the rescue of Diem who declared that the rebels had been thwarted by the 'hand of God'.[34]

With the failure of that right-wing nationalist plot, the initiative passed to Diem's enemies on the left, who provided convenient scapegoats for Diem and his allies in the United States. American officials denied that there were any legitimate grounds for dissatisfaction with the government. They attributed the trouble to a communist campaign of armed action, subversion and terror, instigated and directed by North Vietnam. According to their theory South Vietnam had outstripped the North, particularly in economic growth. Unable to accept that situation, the leaders in Hanoi had 'decided on a course of violence'.[35] In order to see that allegation in perspective we turn now to the developments in North Vietnam in the years following the Geneva Conference.

Four

THE DEVELOPMENT OF THE NORTH: RESISTANCE TO DIEM

Ho Chi Minh, having 'snatched compromise out of the jaws of victory',[1] was faced with a major problem when he returned to Hanoi in October 1954. While he hoped shortly to gain control of the whole of Vietnam, he had in the meanwhile to create a viable political and economic entity in only half a country. That half had, moreover, suffered most in the recent fighting. Even before it was devastated by the conflict between the French and the Vietminh it had been plundered by the Japanese and then in 1946 by the Chinese Nationalists. During the Second World War its roads and railways had been bombed by the US Air Force. Perhaps most serious of all, the area north of the seventeenth parallel was cut off from the main source of its staple diet, rice, which lay in the Mekong Delta. A contemporary French authority on Vietnam, stressing the economic importance of the south, with its large rice surplus and its exports of rubber, pepper, coffee and precious woods, predicted that Ho's regime, deprived of those benefits, would face either starvation or a dependence on Communist China which would be tantamount to annexation.[2]

One of Ho Chi Minh's first priorities was, therefore, the development of agriculture. In the first year of the new government famine was avoided only by a Russian-financed purchase of rice from Burma. The government believed that greater production would be encouraged by a re-allocation of the land. It thus continued a land reform campaign which had begun in the areas controlled by the Vietminh during the war. From 1954 to 1956 the countryside was thrown into chaos as a result of an eruption of violence and terror. The reform was carried out by inexperienced cadres who received little training before being turned loose in the villages. In the villages many people seized the chance to settle old scores.

It has been commonly accepted that thousands of innocent

people were killed and imprisoned; that the brutality of the cadres resulted in a veritable bloodbath. More recently, however, it has been claimed that the source on which much of the discussion of the land reform is based is extremely dubious. According to one view it consists largely of fabrications and serious mistranslations. That view has received support from an unlikely source. In 1972 Nguyen Van Chau, director of the Psychological War Service of the South Vietnamese Armed Forces from 1956 to 1962, stated that the alleged 'Communist bloodbath' was '100 percent fabricated' by US-financed Saigon intelligence services.[3]

Whether or not the slaughter was as terrible as some have alleged, it does appear that the programme got seriously out of hand. The government itself admitted that 'mistakes' had been made and promised corrections. At the end of October 1956 Truong Chinh, the head of the campaign, was replaced as Secretary-General of the Lao Dong Party by Ho Chi Minh. The minister of agriculture was also dismissed. During November the government announced the release of 12,000 people from prison and labour camps. The People's Agricultural Reform Tribunals, which allegedly sentenced many innocent people to death and imprisonment, were abolished. A programme of 'democratization' promised greater freedom of movement, improved living conditions, increased powers for the National Assembly and the holding of elections in 1957.[4] Fitzgerald has argued that the rectification campaign was a remarkable achievement: that it was perhaps the only occasion when a communist leader has admitted that he and his party were in error on a major issue. Taking into account the communist attitude to politics, she points out that the equivalent in the West would be for a leader to confess to treason.[5]

Thanks to the government's change of policy the disaffection gradually subsided. There was of course no return to the old system: the power of the landlords was destroyed. Subsequently it was claimed that the removal of the landlords 'lifted a yoke' from the peasants and released their considerable energies, which the government channelled into agricultural co-operatives.[6] At the end of 1960 there were more than 40,000 co-operatives which included more than 85 per cent of all farming families.[7] After a disastrous beginning the agrarian policy achieved some success. The yield per hectare of raw rice increased. Better

6. North Vietnamese peasants on a collective farm near Haiphong.

hydraulic works and irrigation systems gave more crops per year in each field. Consequently a growth rate of about 3 per cent per annum (a considerable achievement for a developing country) was achieved in the early 1960s. Increasing population meant that the problem of providing enough food remained acute. Starvation, an old scourge of the Vietnamese peasant, was, however, eliminated and a five-year plan for 1961–5 promised further improvement.

The government of North Vietnam intended to have a balanced economy. While they aimed at increasing agricultural production they also pressed ahead with the reconstruction and expansion of industry. Their legacy from the French was not particularly impressive. There were two major industrial enterprises, the cement works at Haiphong and textile plants at Haiphong and Nam Dinh. In addition they had a useful railway system, port installations, a few electric power plants and some other minor factories. Everything was, after a devastating war, in a very poor state of repair. It was fortunate for Ho that considerable foreign aid was made available from the Soviet bloc and China. Between 1955 and 1961 grants and loans totalled more than $1,000,000,000. As a result of the aid and their own efforts the North Vietnamese made significant industrial progress. Buttinger, an American historian, who was for some years a strong supporter of Diem, has commented that, while the masses had to accept austerity, North Vietnam, even before 1960, was 'well on the road toward becoming the most industrialized country of Southeast Asia'. Ho's regime, he noted, had built modern factories and had trained its owned skilled personnel. Less than ten years after its industrialization began it was producing items which were still not being produced in the south: machine tools, electric motors, office equipment, bicycle tyres and even small ocean craft.[8]

In the light of North Vietnam's achievements in industry and agriculture, it is hard to accept the official American view that the communist leaders decided to resort to force in 1959 because they could not take over South Vietnam in any other way and because the south was socially and economically 'far outstripping the North'. That interpretation becomes even more difficult to uphold against the background of other policies pursued by the North Vietnamese.

As already noted, the North Vietnamese government pressed hard for the elections in 1956, only to be ignored by Diem. It continued to urge negotiations on the basis of free general elections by secret ballot in July 1957, March 1958 and as late as July 1959 and 1960. Diem either rebuffed or ignored each initiative, confident that the US would underwrite him. While he knew that the Americans were ready to intervene militarily, his opponents were aware that the help they could expect from their Soviet and Chinese friends would probably be 'restricted to kind words, warm gestures of solidarity, and propaganda campaigns'.[9] The Chinese communists had consistently argued that revolution could not be exported, that the success of revolutionary movements depended on the efforts of the indigenous people. In any case, surrounded as they were by US bases, they were scarcely able to exert much pressure on an ally of America. The Soviet leaders during this period were promoting a policy of peaceful co-existence with the West, and in particular with the United States. Thus they were anxious to reduce tension, not to increase it by impinging on an area where the Americans were, even at this stage, well-entrenched. Furthermore, during the late 1950s a split gradually emerged between China and the Soviet Union. By 1960 it was already pronounced, as was the unlikelihood of any co-ordinated action by both powers on behalf of the North Vietnamese. While both were ready to give aid to the North, they gave little encouragement to a more aggressive policy against Diem.

For some time the consensus, even among the Northern leadership, was opposed to any major move against the government in the south. Ho and his colleagues were, of course, keen to see Vietnam unified under themselves. After 1956, however, they felt that their victory would come later rather than sooner. In January 1957 the National Assembly recognized that 'the struggle for unity would be long and difficult'.[10] An essential first step would be to consolidate the revolution in the north. (Their Soviet allies evidently shared their expectation of a lengthy struggle. At the beginning of 1957 at the United Nations the USSR proposed the simultaneous admission of both Vietnams!) At the end of 1956 the Saigon regime was indeed confident enough to talk of liberating the north where it considered 'the fall of the illegitimate regime was near'.[11]

While the North Vietnamese limited themselves to verbal protests, Diem did not hesitate to use force against the communists. We have already noted some of the consequences of his repression. In the long run it was counter-productive since it provoked a rebellion against him. For a time, however, he seemed fully in control. Major campaigns against the communists in 1956 and 1957 weakened the remnants of the Vietminh in the south. One cadre who survived explained that the official line of the Southern Vietminh from 1954 to 1959 was to carry on a legal, political, non-violent form of struggle. Towards the end of 1959 it allowed 'violence for self-defence'. The first policy – of non-violence – cost the lives of many of his comrades. Nevertheless, despite Diem and the 'strictly legal' line many former Vietminh members were still available for action when the call came.[12]

It appears that during 1959 communist leaders in North and

South Vietnam realized that the time had come to take up arms against Diem: if they were not prepared to give a lead there would be spontaneous uprisings against his rule. In May 1959 the Central Committee of the Lao Dong party voted in favour of fighting 'jointly and severally' for the liberation of Vietnam.[13] Having advised patience and non-violent opposition for several years they were beginning to change their line. They could hardly be accused of being precipitate.

In March 1960 the South Vietnamese 'Veterans of the Resistance association' declared that they were fighting to end the 'Fascist dictatorship of the Ngo family' and to set up 'a democratic government of national union in South Vietnam'. They anticipated that such a government would discuss with North Vietnam how to achieve the peaceful re-unification of the Fatherland.[14] An official from North Vietnam who attended the meeting, reported to Hanoi the strength of popular pressures, warning of a forth-coming struggle which would involve the north. The issue of re-unification and the question of what support should be given to the south were discussed at the Third Congress of the Lao Dong party in September 1960. There it was agreed that more should be done to liberate the South Vietnamese people from imperialism. In addition, Ho Chi Minh gave up the secretaryship of the party in favour of Le Duan who before 1954 had been chief political commissar for the southern guerrillas, thus assuring even closer liaison with the south.[15]

Despite such moves, the congress was not primarily a sabre-rattling occasion. The main Soviet delegate emphasized that peaceful co-existence was the only line completely in accord with the ultimate aim of communism. According to a com-muniqué issued after Soviet–Vietnamese talks which followed the congress, there was complete identity of views on both sides.[16] Such was also the opinion of a staunchly anti-communist commentator who felt the congress had indicated that North Vietnam would follow the Russian policy of peaceful co-existence based on the possibility of avoiding war. It had indeed announced a major defence cut to provide money for economic development.[17]

Our examination of the policies of Ho Chi Minh's government between 1954 and 1960 suggests that they were concerned rather to develop a socialist system in the north than to subvert the regime of Diem in the south. (Although they obviously disliked that regime.) The Saigon–Washington claim that the fighting in South Vietnam, which led to the second Indochina war, was the result of aggression by Hanoi, is not borne out by the evidence. (There is some evidence, indeed that the South was guilty of deploying small saboteur groups against the North.)[18] The outbreak of fighting was in the main provoked by Diem's regime. Naturally the communists did not hesitate to take advantage of his errors and eventually played a major role in the opposition which emerged. To understand the nature of the conflict which followed we must consider what kind of opposition it was.

As already noted, in 1954 the People's Army of Vietnam was regrouped north of the seventeenth parallel. While the regular troops were withdrawn, many other members of the Vietminh remained in the south. Like the organization as a whole, the southern Vietminh were not all communists. There was, however, a hard core of communist cadres who became the leaders of a new resistance movement. By 1958 they had established cells in former Vietminh strongholds: in the U Minh forest at the southern tip of the Mekong Delta, in the jungles to the west of Saigon, in the jungle area of the northern province Quang Nam and elsewhere.[19] Gradually they gained support, moving from their base areas to neighbouring villages where they gathered-in a variety of recruits.

There were those who were quite simply hostile to any government. In many other villages there were branches of the religious sects whom Diem had suppressed. The cadres assiduously fanned their hatred. They also exploited the fact that Diem came from Hué in central Vietnam and that many of his officials were refugees from the north. Southerners themselves, they turned regional animosity to their advantage, keeping in the background the eventual aim of re-unification with their northern comrades. Their best recruiting sergeant was Diem himself. As a result of his brutality, 'the people were like a mound of straw, ready to be ignited'.[20] Included in the combustible material were montagnard tribesmen, forced to leave their traditional homelands to be re-settled in more 'secure' areas, and the many peasants who had been removed from their ancestral villages and forced to live in agrovilles.[21]

Between 1958 and 1960 the cadres were occupied moulding their recruits into resistance groups rather than actively resisting. Before 1959 spontaneous acts of terrorism, including numerous assassinations had been carried out against the official line: towards the end of that year the groups were fully activated. In late September two government battalions were ambushed by guerrillas in the Plain of Reeds, southwest of Saigon. After a brief fight twelve government troops were killed and the rest surrendered. According to Halberstam, it was from this time that the guerrillas became known as the Vietcong.[22] The term 'Vietcong' means 'Vietnamese Communist' and was coined by the Saigon regime as a derogatory description which implied that anyone who fought against Diem was a communist. That implication was unjustified: the opposition was in fact much more widely based.

In December 1960 various oppositionist groups (including communists and non-communists) coalesced to form a National Front for the Liberation of South Vietnam (Mat-Tran dan-Toc giaiphong), commonly known as the National Liberation Front. Somewhere in South Vietnam, perhaps in Tay Ninh province, a hundred delegates representing a dozen or more political parties and religious groups formed a broad coalition, which has been described as 'the Vietminh reborn'.[23] Its objectives, specified in a ten-point programme, were nationalist rather than Marxist. Just as the Vietminh had emphasized opposition to French colonialism, so the NLF called for the overthrow of 'the camouflaged colonial regime' established by the USA. Disregarding the tensions that existed between Diem and the Americans, the Front attacked the 'servile', Yankee-dominated regime in the south. Their aim was to replace Diem with a government, representing all social classes, nationalities and religions, to be formed from the anti-Diemist parties. The new government would ensure essential democratic liberties, including the right of all patriotic organizations, whatever their politics, to carry on normal activities. It would also improve living conditions and implement land reform.

The new government was to pursue a neutralist foreign policy. Diplomatic relations would be established with all countries, regardless of their political complexion. Furthermore, South Vietnam was to remain outside all power blocs and to refuse any military alliance. The most crucial issue of foreign policy was the relationship with North Vietnam. Point IX of the Front's programme advocated the peaceful re-unification of both zones by stages 'on the basis of negotiations and through the seeking of ways and means in conformity with the interests of the Vietnamese nation'.[24]

Political programmes are notoriously unreliable as predictors of actual as opposed to proposed policy. Any programme in which there was communist participation was doubly suspect. Thus the NLF programme, and indeed the whole movement, was simply dismissed by Diem and his US allies as a convenient cover for Hanoi. They failed to perceive that the emergence of the Front marked not a mass shift to Marxism but a crisis of confidence within South Vietnam. The nature of that crisis becomes clearer if we focus our attention on the villages.

We have seen that the North Vietnamese put land reform at the top of their agenda. It appeared to be a bloody business until the government intervened at the end of 1956 to 'correct' some of the 'errors'.[25] Nevertheless it did finally end the rule of the landlords, which was the necessary first step to improving the lot of the peasants. Wherever landlordism survives so also does peasant discontent. Under Diem the landlords did not merely survive but positively thrived. They first delayed then emasculated land reform in South Vietnam. Nothing at all was attempted in 1954; in 1955 a few tentative moves were made to safeguard tenants' rights. Not until 1956 was there any significant distribution of land. Even then the programme was balked and five years after it began over a million tenants had received no land at all. Many other peasants were aggrieved at having to pay for land they considered their own. Under the Vietminh, large landowners had been dispossessed. Under Diem, peasants who had been given their land were obliged to pay for it at rates they could not afford. Buttinger has pointed out that, while Diem had the power to eradicate landlordism, he was too conservative to do so. Such a drastic social change was repugnant to him; instead he helped the landlords to keep the peasants in subjection.[26]

As opposition in the countryside grew, Diem appointed his own officials to maintain contact with and control over the villages. They personified the government's intrusion into the lives of its citizens – an intrusion alien to Vietnamese tradition. For centuries the villages, under the direction of their own notables, had met the demands of the central authority without undue external supervision and from a sense of obligation to the emperor. The villagers felt no such obligation to Diem who simply coerced them into obedience.

The consequence of his heavy-handed conservatism was a widening gap in the countryside between the rulers and the ruled. The status and influence of those who had given the villages some sense of community had been eroded. Instead, the regime attempted to impose cohesion by force, thus inviting the formation of a counter-élite to occupy the vacuum it had created. The communist cadres and other NLF leaders did what Diem's officials neglected to do. They listened to the grievances of the peasants and, having gained their confidence, persuaded many of them that the remedy was to build a new kind of society. During a period of discord and dissension they offered a new consensus. What made Diem's regime particularly vulnerable to their approach was not merely the reaction to its use of terror but also the fact that, in so many ways, it was simply failing in its duty as a government. Unlike the old traditional system on the one hand and the NLF at the other end of the political spectrum, Diem's clique failed to establish any rapport with the Vietnamese people.

Having forged its links with the people, the NLF was able to organize an increasingly effective opposition. While Diem managed to crush the revolt of his own troops in November 1960, he could not prevent the countryside going over to his enemies. By mid-1961 US intelligence services reported that NLF membership had reached 15,000, half of whom were fully armed.[27] Shortly after he took office President Kennedy learned from his experts that large areas of the countryside in South Vietnam were 'under considerable Communist control' and that the Vietcong were encircling Saigon itself. There was a widespread feeling that Diem was unable to rally his people against the communists because of his 'reliance on virtual one-man rule, his toleration of corruption . . . and his refusal to relax a rigid system of public controls'.[28] How to achieve American goals in Vietnam with such an unpromising ally was a major problem for the new President.

Five

KENNEDY AND THE GROWING AMERICAN INVOLVEMENT

President Kennedy accepted the objectives in Vietnam laid down by his predecessors. He reiterated the claim that the United States' main purpose was to preserve South Vietnam's independence. In his first State of the Union message he reminded his fellow-citizens of the threat of international communism: '. . . in Asia, the relentless pressures of the Chinese Communists menace the security of the entire area – from the borders of India and South Viet Nam to the jungles of Laos . . .'[1] Thus, he argued, the US commitment to 'Free Vietnam' was intended not only to preserve the independence of the South Vietnamese but also to maintain America's prestige and influence as the chief bastion of the whole 'Free World'. In the latter part of his presidency Kennedy expressed in private some reservations about the US role in Asia. All his public statements, however, emphasized the importance of taking a stand in Vietnam.

During his first months in office he was even more forceful in private than in his public pronouncements. On 11 May 1961 he ordered the deployment of 400 'Special Forces' in South Vietnam, together with 100 other US advisers. Those moves were not disclosed to the public, nor was his decision to begin a secret war against North Vietnam. Intelligence agents were covertly infiltrated into the North, sabotage teams established and leaflets dropped by air incited the people to rise against their leaders. Teams were also sent to Southeast Laos to attack Vietcong bases and lines of communication. In addition, American advisers trained the South Vietnamese army to carry out 'ranger' raids against the North.[2] At the beginning of the Kennedy administration Khrushchev, the Soviet leader, had made a major speech in favour of wars of national liberation which was interpreted, probably mistakenly, as a challenge to the United States. Suddenly, one observer noted, 'the stopping of guerrilla warfare became a great fad.' Kennedy

7. **An American adviser on patrol with South Vietnamese troops.**

himself became fascinated with unconventional warfare and considered that counter-guerrilla and counter-revolutionary training would pay handsome dividends. The Vietcong would, he thought, be beaten at their own game, and at quite a modest cost.[3]

He failed to understand that what made the guerrillas a formidable force was the support they drew from the people. Their capacity to convince the peasants that they were both fighting the same fight was their great strength. Their skill at living in the jungle and in mounting ambushes was important but secondary. Such skills might be acquired at the Special Warfare School at Fort Bragg; there was, however, no course which could teach the GIs to win the trust of Vietnamese peasants.

Experiments with special forces were in the main ineffectual and were not enough to satisfy the US military establishment. Throughout the summer and autumn of 1961 Kennedy was under pressure to send American ground combat troops against the Vietcong. The situation was undoubtedly serious, as General Maxwell Taylor, the President's special military adviser, reported after a fact-finding mission to South Vietnam. Taylor recommended sending US troops to raise national morale in the South and to show other countries in Southeast Asia that America was determined to resist a communist takeover. He believed that Americans could give the South Vietnamese army 'the élan and style needed to win'. A price would be paid for those benefits: the presence of US combat troops would increase international tension and accentuate the risk of a major war in Asia.[4] While Kennedy's generals were sure the price was worth paying, he had some doubts. He appreciated that having given way once, he would soon be asked to send even more men. 'It's like taking a drink,' he said. 'The effect wears off, and you have to take another.'[5]

Nevertheless, he did give in partially to the demands of the military. In November 1961 he agreed to send more support troops and advisers, while still demurring at the use of combat units. At the end of 1960 US forces in Vietnam numbered 773; by the end of 1963 there were 16,500. Inevitably the advisers and support troops were involved in actual combat. The numbers of Americans killed and wounded rose from 14 in 1961 to 109 in 1962 and then to 489 in 1963. In addition to more men Kennedy also provided more materials of war, including helicopters and other aircraft.[6]

Superficially there appeared to be little change in US policy – rather more of the same mixture. The theory was still that the South Vietnamese should be helped to help themselves, without involving too deeply the United States. Once again, as in 1954 under Eisenhower, the administration tried to ensure that their money was being well spent. The increased help was made conditional on concrete demonstrations by Diem that he was 'prepared to work in an orderly way . . . and broaden the political base of the regime'. Kennedy's actions seemed to be minor variations on a well-worn theme.[7]

Retrospectively, however, it has been claimed that Kennedy transformed the 'limited-risk gamble' of the Eisenhower years into a 'broad commitment' to prevent the communist domination of South Vietnam.[8] There is some truth in that judgment. In refusing to send combat troops, Kennedy felt that he had acted moderately and that he was therefore justified in being aggressive in his speeches, thus satisfying different shades of opinion in the

USA. In his public statements on Vietnam he 'markedly escalated the rhetoric and the rationale for being there'.[9] They had the effect of moving the Vietnam war nearer the forefront of American politics and of encouraging the generals, who were adept at seizing their chances, to seek a greater share in the shaping of policy. Their pressure had already helped to increase US spending considerably and had put many more men into the battle zones. During 1962 they pressed their demands at a number of points.

8. An American helicopter bringing in supplies to a South Vietnamese village.

They requested new jet planes for use in Vietnam; on this issue the President did not accommodate them. They also wanted free-fire zones (initially areas where unused bombs could be jettisoned), unrestricted use of napalm and widespread defoliation of the enemy's jungle refuges. Kennedy was doubtful about those demands; in particular he was appalled by the use of napalm against living targets. Nevertheless, the generals succeeded in winning his consent for a restricted use of napalm (who could monitor that restriction?), for defoliation against lines of communication and for limited free-fire zones.[10] We can see here the early stages of the process whereby the US military began effectively to determine policy in Vietnam. Despite his reservations, Kennedy found it increasingly difficult to resist his generals once he had opened the door to them.

The long-term effects of his policy were to be felt during President Johnson's administration. One of the short-term results was the tightening of the bonds that linked the US government with the Diem regime. Attempts to impose conditions on the help he received were futile while he was the only viable anti-communist leader in the South. As one American journalist succinctly commented, the United States was bound to 'sink or swim with Ngo Dinh Diem'.[11] Continuing to support Diem and also allowing more initiative to US military leaders were policies which complemented each other. Under Diem there was no prospect of political reform. Thus there could be only a military response to a worsening situation. Kennedy's zeal for counter-insurgency and fashionable discussion about winning over the 'hearts and minds' of the Vietnamese people created the illusion that his administration saw the problem as essentially political. The fact is that only lip-service was paid to the importance of the political situation, as was demonstrated by the Strategic Hamlets Programme.

The objectives of that programme were to cut off the guerrillas from the peasants on whose support they relied and, at the same time, give the peasants the 'security' to allow them to choose 'freely' between the South Vietnamese government and the Vietcong. It resembled the 'agroville' scheme, started in 1959, whereby Diem planned to resettle about three hundred thousand peasants over a period of some four years. The agrovilles were fortified reserves where the peasants would no longer be accessible to the guerrillas. They drew their inspiration from the successful resettlement of the Chinese 'squatters' by the British during the Malayan emergency. As we have seen, the situation in Vietnam was very different from Malaya.[12] Whereas the British had to cope with a comparatively small-scale resettlement, the Diem regime, with its customary ineptitude, started a much more ambitious scheme. Almost without exception, the agrovilles failed in their objective. Apart from the gross corruption and inefficiency of its champions, the whole scheme was under-financed and had not taken into account the depth of peasant resentment. Its consequences were greater discontent in the countryside and a boost to the resistance movement.

Despite that fiasco, a new resettlement programme, based on the notion of strategic hamlets, was devised – according to Bernard Fall, 'the most mammoth example of "social engineering" in the non-Communist world'.[13] Launched in the Mekong Delta early in 1962, by August it extended throughout the whole country. At the end of September the regime claimed that over one-third of the total rural population had been resettled. There were indeed many so-called strategic hamlets. Provincial officials, terrified of offending Nhu (who posed as the scheme's originator) and anxious to receive US aid earmarked for the programme, competed to build as many as possible. One American wryly commented that if you stood still long enough they would 'throw a piece of barbed wire around you and call you a strategic hamlet'.[14] Quantitatively they may have seemed impressive: in every other respect they were, like the agrovilles, a total failure.

The villagers were almost always resettled forcibly, sometimes being pushed at gunpoint into the 'security' of the hamlets. Areas surrounding the hamlets were declared 'open zones' where aerial and artillery bombardment served as an extra inducement to move into the hamlet and stay there. While the scheme helped to line the pockets of the provincial chiefs and gave Diem the illusion of controlling his own people, the people themselves suffered great hardship. For them, the programme entailed, in the words of a US Marine Colonel, 'forced resettlement, physical oppression, coercion, and political "persuasion" by the club'.[15] The first of those was the worst. Vietnamese peasants worshipped their ancestors and expressed their reverence by tending ancestral graves. The land where they lay was sacred and formed part of the peasants' social identity. When they were driven from that land the links with their ancestors were snapped. They felt totally lost in a strange world, although geographically it may not have been very distant from their own village. Their feeling of disorientation often produced results diametrically opposed to those intended. Fitzgerald has pointed out that forced resettlement might drive a peasant 'off the edges of his old life', thus exposing him directly to 'the political movement that could best provide him with a new

9. A North Vietnamese anti-aircraft unit.

identity'.[16] Even those who did not join the guerrillas were, by the very act of relocation, turned against the government.

Many did join the Vietcong. Ironically, one of the alleged aims of the Strategic Hamlets Programme had been to allow the peasants a 'free choice' between the government and its opponents. An American official later commented that one of the reasons for its failure was that Vietcong supporters and agents had managed to remain in the hamlets and continue their subversion. Clearly that was disastrous: there could be no 'free choice' between the government and the communists while the Vietcong were allowed to exist![17]

They were not merely existing: their numbers were increasing. An American intelligence memorandum at the end of 1962 – when one third of South Vietnam's peasants were supposedly safely ensconced in strategic hamlets – stated that the Vietcong had 'expanded the size and enhanced the capability and organization of its guerrilla force'.[18] Since January its élite troops had grown from some 16,500 to about 23,000, supported by some 100,000 irregulars. Although the government mustered about 285,000 men, including regulars and para-military groups, they could not prevent the Vietcong controlling about one-fifth of the villages and infiltrating the urban areas. As one observer remarked, the circle of artillery and barbed wire around the strategic hamlets 'enclosed a political void that waited for the NLF'.[19] By the beginning of 1963, according to official US figures, about half the population of South Vietnam supported the National Liberation Front. Such statistics were tucked away in confidential reports. In public all was said to be going well – the strategic hamlets were undermining the VC and the guerrilla war was being won by the government forces. Those dangerous illusions were fostered by, among others, a man who might have been expected to sound the alarm.

General Paul D. Harkins was appointed head of the US Military Advisory Command (MACV) in January 1962. On his arrival at Saigon he told reporters that he was an optimist and that he intended to have optimists on his staff.[20] Under his direction, information was processed to provide the success stories that would please his superiors in Washington. Officers filing pessimistic reports were sacked and their statements suppressed. Critical journalists were upbraided and told to 'get on the team'. Under Diem the war was being lost. Instead of trying to correct the faults, the US Embassy in Saigon and MACV joined with Diem's officials in pretending that the VC were at the end of their tether. Harkins was a man of 'compelling mediocrity' who was carrying out what he conceived as his orders. His talented superiors were even more at fault.

Maxwell Taylor, Chairman of the Joint Chiefs of Staff from 1962 to 1964, consistently supported his old friend Harkins. Having been responsible for appointing Harkins to MACV, he was perhaps unwilling to admit his own mistake. Robert McNamara, the Secretary of Defense, who later was to comment that Harkins 'wasn't worth a damn', proved to be as gullible as Taylor. A great expert in evaluating data, McNamara simply accepted all the distorted statistics from Saigon and naturally got the wrong answer. On his numerous visits to Vietnam he failed to see even what was in front of him. His trips, carefully arranged by Harkins to show the bright side, gave McNamara an illusion of knowledge rather than a genuine understanding of the situation.[21]

While Diem and his US allies deluded themselves, partly because they could not afford to face the truth, the people of South Vietnam had no reason to close their eyes to what was happening. They saw that the regime was under increasing strain, with opposition groups beginning to assert themselves in the towns. The government itself was aware of that particular danger and determined to nip protest in the bud. Hence the crisis which eventually brought the downfall of Diem.

It began on 8 May 1963 when government troops in Hué opened fire on militant Buddhists demonstrating against restrictions imposed on their celebration of the anniversary of Buddah's birth. Nine people were killed and several crushed by an armoured car. The government claimed that the deaths and injuries were caused by a grenade thrown into the crowd by an agent of the Vietcong. Even after the true account had been widely circulated it persisted with its lie. Conciliation was not the strong suit of Diem's regime and as the crisis deepened it remained intransigent. Any attempt at compromise would, it felt, be interpreted as weakness.

The Buddhists demanded that the government admit its responsibility for the deaths and pay compensation to the victims' families. When that was refused they began to agitate against the regime. Apart from the issue of compensation they had other reasons for resenting Diem: a Catholic himself he had favoured his co-religionists and discriminated against the Buddhists since 1955. Even religious grievances were only one aspect of the widespread and increasingly vocal hostility to the government. As a Vietnamese academic pointed out during the crisis, the people of Vietnam were no strangers to oppression. They were used to biding their time and when the right time came they found ways of expressing themselves. Since under Diem they did not dare make outright political protests, they gave vent to their feeling through religion.[22] Thanks to Diem's stubbornness and the political acumen of the Buddhist leaders, what might have passed off as a minor incident broadened into a full-scale confrontation.

The most dramatic and harrowing event of the Buddhists' protest was the self-immolation of the monk Thich Quang Duc. On 11 June 1963, seated in the lotus position, he burned himself to death in the centre of Saigon. Halberstam, an eye-witness, recorded: 'Flames were coming from a human being; his body was

10. A Buddhist monk burns himself in protest against the policies of the South Vietnamese government.

slowly withering and shrivelling up, his head blackening and char-
ring . . . As he burned he never moved a muscle, never uttered a
sound, his outward composure in sharp contrast to the wailing
people around him . . . All around this scene of medieval horror
were the signs of modern times: a young Buddhist priest with a
microphone saying calmly over and over again in Vietnamese and
English, "A Buddhist priest burns himself to death. A Buddhist
priest becomes a martyr."[23] Madame Nhu dismissed the incident
as a 'barbecue' and her husband later commented that if the
Buddhists wished to stage another one he would be 'glad to supply
the gasoline'.[24] In Vietnam and throughout the world millions of
people were horrified by the burning and the callousness of the
Nhus' reaction to it. The American leadership, staggered by the
event and its consequences, attempted to exert pressure on Diem
to make him come to terms with the Buddhists.

There was, however, little chance of reconciliation between
the Buddhists and their growing number of supporters on the one
hand and Diem on the other. Thich Quang Duc had made a remarkable gesture of protest; the response to it prompted his fellow
Buddhists to press home their attack. The regime, in particular the
Nhus, were determined to crush them once for all. While the
Buddhists made the running the government made the mistakes.
Its behaviour was so inept that, in the eyes of one observer, it
appeared to be 'trying to commit suicide'.[25] Perhaps its most
suicidal act was to order raids against Buddhist pagodas by Special
Force troops controlled by Ngo Dinh Nhu.

They launched the attack in a typically underhand way. On
15 August Diem claimed that he had always been in favour of
conciliating the Buddhists. That statement may have been, in part,
a farewell gift for the US ambassador, Nolting, who had since his
appointment in 1961 consistently supported the regime. Guided
by a misplaced sense of duty rather than any reasoned appraisal of
the situation, he had turned a blind eye to all its faults. At the time
of the summer crisis he hoped to refurbish the 'image' of the Ngo
family by urging a reconciliation with the Buddhists. That hope
was soon dashed. Within a week of his departure from Vietnam
he was made to look the fool that he was. On 21 August pagodas
in Saigon, Hué and many other cities were raided and thousands
of monks arrested; some were killed and many of them beaten.
The raids offended not only the Buddhists but also the army,

members of the government itself and also the Americans.[26]

The generals were affronted because Nhu had dressed his special forces as paratroops in order to lay the blame for the raids on the army. Within two days General Le Van Kim was urging the Americans to take a stand against the Nhus to enable the army to displace them.[27] Civilian officials also urged their immediate removal. Diem's defence minister warned the United States not to acquiesce in what they had done; the foreign minister resigned and shaved his head like a Buddhist monk in protest.[28] Many Americans were ready to heed their criticisms. They were appalled by the brutality of the raids and considered the repudiation of Diem's solemn word to Nolting a 'slap in the face for the US'.[29]

For a number of those who directed American policy the pagoda strikes were the last straw. Thereafter they were prepared to disembarrass themselves from Ngo Dinh Nhu and his wife – an action which, given the solidarity of the Ngo family, would precipitate the removal of Diem himself. Henry Cabot Lodge, Nolting's replacement as ambassador, felt it would be disastrous to persist with a totally discredited regime. Less than forty-eight hours after arriving at Saigon he informed the State Department that high ranking Vietnamese generals were sounding out possible American reaction to a coup against Diem. State's reply on 24 August made it clear that the US government could not tolerate a situation in which power continued to lie in Nhu's hands. Diem was to be given a chance to replace Nhu and his coterie. If he refused the US would be forced to consider his own removal and Lodge was instructed to 'urgently examine all possible alternative leadership and make detailed plans as to how we might bring about Diem's replacement if this should become necessary'. State went on to explain that there could be no detailed instructions from Washington about the operation: whatever action Lodge took would be 'backed to the hilt'.[30]

On 29 August Lodge informed Secretary of State Rusk that he agreed with the new line, pointing out that it clearly meant the overthrow of the Diem government. There could be no turning back, he remarked, since US prestige was in large measure already committed to that end and would be even more so as the facts leaked out. Furthermore, said Lodge, there was no possibility that the war could be won under Diem's leadership, nor was there any longer even the slightest prospect that Diem might 'govern the country in a way to gain the support of the people who count . . .'[31] However, despite Lodge's evident apparent eagerness to be rid of the government, the Vietnamese generals made no immediate move.

They could hardly be blamed. For nine years the Americans had backed Diem and when, almost overnight, they changed their tune the generals were nonplussed. Over the years they had learned a healthy respect for Ngo Dinh Nhu and suspected that the latest crisis might be another of his tricks, a manoeuvre to flush out the dissidents in the ranks of the regime. There had always been a close link between Nhu and the US Central Intelligence Agency. How then could the generals trust CIA agents who promised support for a coup to deprive the Ngo family of its power? Fearing betrayal they stood pat. On 31 August Lodge reported to Washington that the conspiracy against Diem had collapsed since the generals had neither the will nor the organization to accomplish anything.[32] To a friend he suggested: 'Perhaps they are like the rest of us, and are afraid to die.'[33] Also on 31 August the National Security Council met in Washington. With the concurrence of Vice-President Johnson and Secretary of Defense McNamara, Rusk insisted that US policy be based on two points: first, they would not pull out of Vietnam until the war was won; secondly, they would not organize a coup against Diem.[34]

The fact was that by the beginning of September US policy regarding Vietnam was in complete disarray, with its leadership divided and in a quandary. Kennedy was as confused as the rest. He was still stuck with Diem while recognizing that he was a hopeless liability. In a television interview on 2 September he suggested that changes in policy and personnel were needed for Diem to regain popular support and improve his chances of winning the war.[35] Various attempts were made to enforce such changes on him. On 14 September the US government announced that it was deferring action on a programme, costing $18.5 million, to finance commercial imports into South Vietnam. Subsequently it suspended such subsidies for trade, imposed a freeze on loans and ceased unconditional financial support for Nhu's special forces.[36]

Although these moves were not announced in public, they were soon well known in Saigon, a city 'keyed-up and alert to every nuance in American policy'. Whatever the precise intentions of the

11. **Saigon civilians huddle behind tanks during the overthrow of Ngo Dinh Diem.**

US leaders, their pressure campaign was bound to encourage those who thought of toppling Diem; the regime itself accused Washington of sabotaging the war effort. During the month of October the generals gradually screwed their courage to the sticking place, convincing themselves that the Americans were indeed serious about supporting a coup. For their part the US leaders were still divided on the issue, although the forces in favour of a coup were becoming stronger. The thinking in Washington was reflected in a message on 30 October from McGeorge Bundy, Kennedy's special assistant for national security, to Lodge. On one hand it warned him to dissuade the generals if he felt that there was not 'clearly a high prospect of success'. However Bundy also stated that 'once a coup under responsible leadership has begun . . . it is in the interest of the US Government that it should succeed'.[37]

In Saigon the time for equivocation had passed. Shortly after 1 p.m. on 1 November the plotters began to take over the city. They seized police headquarters, the radio stations, the airport and attacked the presidential palace and the special forces barracks. Except at the palace, resistance was crushed within three hours. Eventually Diem and Nhu escaped from the palace through a secret tunnel and hid in Cholon, the Chinese section of Saigon. On the morning of 2 November, having been promised safe conduct out of the country, they were instead tracked down and summarily shot to death in the back of an armoured personnel carrier.

With Diem dead US policy in Vietnam had to be re-defined. Another result of his death was that people could at last tell the truth about how badly the war was going for the government. Even Lodge, who was expecting bad news, was shocked at how discouraging it was. On 21 November he left for Washington to inform the President that the situation was much worse than they had thought. At San Francisco he learned that John Kennedy had been shot dead at Dallas. The Vietnam War had become the responsibility of Lyndon Johnson.

Six

JOHNSON'S WAR

Lodge's revelations about the failure of the Strategic Hamlets Programme and the ineffectiveness of the counter-insurgency campaign produced an uncompromising response from the new American President. 'I am not,' affirmed Johnson, 'going to lose Vietnam.' Nor did he intend to allow Southeast Asia 'go the way China went'.[1] Within four days of taking office he confirmed US support for Diem's successors and requested plans for clandestine operations against the government in the North.[2] In December he reviewed the whole situation as presented in a report from McNamara who had returned from a visit to Vietnam with a belatedly realistic appraisal of the war.

McNamara, still Secretary of Defense, found the new government in Saigon inexperienced and indecisive and that the US establishment there was functioning badly, partly as a result of tensions between Lodge and Harkins. The enemy, on the other hand, had, since the death of Diem, grown even more formidable. The Vietcong dominated a number of key provinces where they had destroyed many strategic hamlets and replaced government officials with their own men who 'collected taxes at will'. McNamara advised the President to run scared, 'hoping for the best, but preparing for more forceful moves'.[3] In January the Joint Chiefs of Staff urged him to increase the pressure on the enemy, arguing that the Vietnam War was assuming global significance and that the United States should no longer pull any punches. While welcoming the proposed covert actions against the North, they warned that a much higher 'level of activity' was necessary to impress both friend and foe.[4] A greater degree of American control and more extensive action against North Vietnam were two of their proposals which were soon implemented. Meanwhile the elaborate programme of clandestine actions against the North, code-named Operation Plan 34A, began on 1 February.

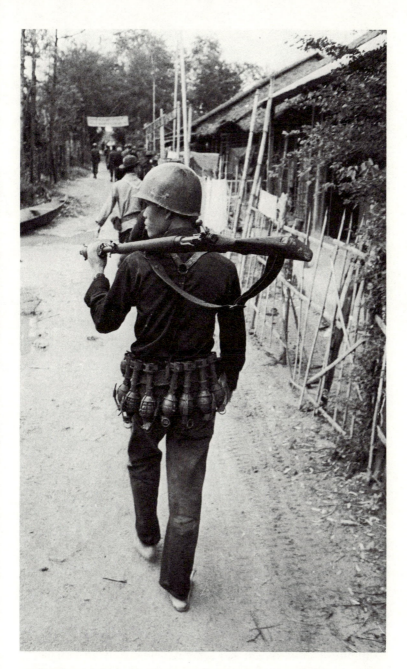

12. Members of the South Vietnamese 'Popular Force' on patrol in a strategic hamlet.

Included in the programme, which was of course concealed from the public, were U-2 spy-plane flights over North Vietnam, kidnapping North Vietnamese for intelligence information, dropping sabotage teams to blow up rail and road bridges and bombarding coastal installations from PT boats. The operations were planned by the US and Saigon authorities and carried out by South Vietnamese or 'hired personnel' (Asian mercenaries). Control of the whole plan lay in the hands of General Harkins. At the same time, destroyer patrols, code-named De Soto patrols, began to collect information about North Vietnamese radar and coastal defences in the Gulf of Tonkin. Yet another measure was an intensification of air operations in Laos, one of Vietnam's western neighbours.

The purpose of all such activity was to tighten the pressure on the leaders of North Vietnam. It was hoped that they in turn would seek relief by exerting their influence on the NLF to end the insurgency in the South. Rostow, chairman of the State Department Policy Planning Council, and one of the government's leading intellectuals, argued that the revolution in the South could be 'dried up' by cutting off its external sources of support and supply.[5] Thus when it became evident that the 34A operations were having little effect, the possible bombing of the North appeared on the agenda, although almost a year elapsed before full-scale attacks were launched. The way was, as we shall see, carefully prepared before the big decision was taken. However, while there was some agonizing over issues of timing and possible international consequences, there was virtually no questioning of the main 'justification' for a bombing offensive – that the North was responsible for the war in the South.

The presumption of Northern guilt was clear in the National Security Council memorandum agreed by Johnson on 26 November 1963. In order to defend the new measures against the North it directed the State Department to produce a documented case 'to demonstrate to the world the degree to which the Viet Cong is controlled, sustained and supplied from Hanoi'.[6] Eventually, in February 1965, State published a White Paper making the allegations used to justify US bombing. 'In Viet Nam,' it declared, 'a Communist government has set out deliberately to conquer a sovereign people in a neighbouring state.'[7] The authors had, however, some difficulty in finding convincing evidence for their accusation. One, who was responsible for gathering proof of infiltration from the North, later commented that the document was a 'dismal disappointment' and that 'the actual findings seemed pretty frail'.[8] Not only were they pretty frail, they were contradicted by other American sources, even by the State Department itself. In June 1964 its Director of Intelligence pointed out that not only were most of the Vietcong South Vietnamese but also that most of their weapons came not from communist countries but from capture, purchase or local manufacture.[9] The failure of the White Paper to make its case was immediately publicized in a detailed reply to it written by an independent journalist, I. F. Stone.[10] Subsequently, information in the Pentagon Papers undermined other arguments which attempted to justify the bombing campaign.

One such argument was advanced, after the US had already escalated the war, by Secretary of State Rusk. He claimed, in a Senate Hearing, that the North Vietnamese had moved their 325th Division into South Vietnam before the bombing started.[11] The Pentagon analyst, however, has shown that, when the order to bomb was finally issued in February 1965, the US knew of no regular Northern military units in the South.[12] Rusk, like the President and other policy makers, had the facility of ignoring facts which clashed with their own preconceptions. To manufacture acceptable reasons for the US bombing it was necessary to believe that they were responding to intolerable pressure from the other side. The fact that the evidence for such pressure was insubstantial was simply ignored.

However, the Johnson administration had not merely to convince themselves that escalation was necessary. They also had to prepare the American people for a significant and costly extension of the war effort in Southeast Asia. In fact they had to be educated to accept that events had transformed the war from one in which Vietnamese could be left to fight each other, with the US supporting the 'good' Vietnamese, into a conflict which demanded direct participation by the United States. During the last decade Vietnam has been such a dominant issue in American politics that it takes an effort to recall that in 1964 it was only one of many issues. Few Americans outside government circles knew what was happening in Vietnam. Even fewer were anxious to increase the US commitment there. The major topic in 1964 was the Presidential election and the indications were that most Americans wanted a president who would not embroil them in a major war in Asia. A convincing victory in the election was Johnson's principal concern. Every issue was to be handled with that objective in mind – including the issue of Vietnam. The President required McNamara 'to keep Vietnam in hand and tidy it up'.[13] Within the administration discussion of the war was limited; only the very top people were involved in the decisions.

The tenor of the confidential debate was that a more forceful US policy should be pursued in Vietnam at 'an appropriate moment'. All the major policy makers agreed with McNamara's statement of US objectives in South Vietnam. In effect he postulated the right of the USA to defeat the revolution there by 'economic and social pressures' together with 'police and military help'. He claimed that the conflict was seen by the rest of the world as a 'test case of US capacity to help a nation meet a Communist "war of liberation"'.[14] There was no doubting the terrible consequences of American failure. Vietnam, Laos and Cambodia would probably be dominated by 'Communism'. Obliged to 'accommodate to Communism', Burma would cease to be an American sphere of influence. Thailand would soon be under pressure. The Philippines would become vulnerable and the 'threat' would be greatly increased to the following: India, Australia and New Zealand, Taiwan, Korea and Japan.[15]

McNamara's memorandum, so specific in some respects, revealed considerable confusion as to who the enemy was and about the precise nature of the threat. Was he referring to Soviet Communism, Chinese Communism or the Communism of North Vietnam? Which brand threatened which country? Was he contending, for example, that New Zealand was menaced by the North Vietnamese? There was a question also regarding the definition of a 'Communist war of liberation'. Such a war, according to the view from the Left, was one in which indigenous revolutionaries were in conflict with the established government of a country and its imperial protectors. McNamara's document implied that it was a war in which an external Communist power (North Vietnam in this case) imposed a Communist regime on another country with the help of a fifth column (the Vietcong).

Since 1945 American leaders had constantly invoked the menace of an international Communist conspiracy directed from Moscow and, after 1949, also from Peking. In the wake of the Sino–Soviet split that particular (but unparticularized) threat ceased to be credible. What remained was a scarcely identifiable adversary, a rather mysterious but dangerous force, difficult to specify in any concrete terms.[16] From the memorandum it is, however, possible to deduce why that vague force could cause such perturbation in Washington. Clearly, McNamara believed that it threatened to undermine the influence of the United States, denying to the Americans their 'right' to apply economic and military pressure to maintain their dominant status in the world, their 'super-powerdom'. While the precise nature of the international communist enemy was rather conjectural the US response was definite enough: a massive military commitment in Southeast Asia.

The North Vietnamese were identified as the most urgent danger to US dominance and preparations were made to deal with them when the right moment came or could be contrived. In April the Joint Chiefs of Staff approved a plan for 'retaliatory' (sic) air-strikes within 72 hours and for full-scale bombing of the North on 30 days' notice. The plan stated how many planes and what bomb tonnages would be required and provided a list of targets with the damage to be inflicted. At the same time an estimate was made of possible Chinese and North Vietnamese reactions, together with the number of American ground forces needed to cope with them. The air-war scenario specified that on D-Day −30 there should be a 'Presidential speech in general terms launching [a] Joint Resolution' [of Congress].[17] William Bundy, Assistant Secretary of State for Far Eastern Affairs, in fact drafted the Congressional resolution on 25 May – the resolution which was finally put to Congress in August, after the Gulf of Tonkin incident.[18]

It was considered inappropriate to tell the Congress or the American people how much was being done for their protection. Johnson eagerly anticipated contending against Barry Goldwater in the November election when he would present himself as the reasonable man of the centre, the master of consensus politics, against the wild man of the Republican right. Goldwater exposed himself to attack because of his bellicose attitudes. While he did not actually advocate nuclear war, he talked so much about it that he appeared as an irresponsible war-monger. He did in fact favour an air-war against North Vietnam. To gain maximum leverage from Goldwater's bellicosity, Johnson had to conceal

13. **Phom Van Dong, North Vietnamese prime minister, with British journalist James Cameron in Hanoi.**

the fact that he himself was preparing to bomb the North. He did so very effectively and was publicly proclaimed as the peace candidate while privately making cautious but definite steps towards a wider war.

In June the administration implemented one of the proposals

in the April air-war scenario: that an intermediary should tell Hanoi that the US was determined to protect South Vietnam. Seaborn, the Canadian representative on the International Control Commission, secretly met the North Vietnamese Prime Minister at the request of the US government. He informed Pham Van Dong that American patience was not limitless. The United States 'knew' the control exercised by the North over the Vietcong and warned that any escalation by the Vietcong would result in 'the greatest devastation' of North Vietnam itself.[19] Disregarding that warning, the guerrillas persisted, with great success, in attacking the military regime in Saigon. With an intemperance born of despair General Khanh, the South Vietnamese leader, boasted publicly that he would invade the North. The US felt obliged to reassure its demoralized ally. On 24 July Khanh was told confidentially that the Americans might themselves attack the North if the pressure on his government became excessive.[20] The Joint Chiefs in fact proposed air strikes against the North by unmarked planes flown by non-American crews. Before their proposal could be considered it was overtaken by events.

On 31 July South Vietnamese naval commandos, part of the 34A programme, attacked the North Vietnamese islands Hon Me and Hon Nieu in the Gulf of Tonkin. Shortly afterwards, on 2 August, the US destroyer *Maddox*, which was engaged on a De Soto intelligence gethering patrol, was attacked by North Vietnamese torpedo boats. Two were damaged by planes from the nearby aircraft-carrier *Ticonderoga*, the third was sunk by the *Maddox*. Johnson, on 3 August, ordered the *Maddox*, supported by another destroyer the *C. Turner Joy*, to return to the Tonkin Gulf. A second carrier, the *Constellation*, joined the *Ticonderoga*. During the night of 4 August both destroyers signalled that they were under attack. Because of the Pacific time-difference, news of the incident reached Washington in mid-morning on the 4th. By 1.25 p.m. the Chiefs of Staff had recommended that fighter-bombers from *Ticonderoga* and *Constellation* should retaliate by attacking four North Vietnamese torpedo-boat bases and an oil-storage depot. Having approved the raids, Johnson met Congressional leaders from both parties to outline the day's events and to request a resolution approving his policy. They promised support for what the President had described as a 'limited retaliation'. While the aircraft were heading for their targets Johnson informed the American people on television that the actions taken had been a 'fitting' response which accorded with 'the highest tradition of the United States Navy'.[21]

The next day McNamara reported that twenty-five North Vietnamese patrol craft had been destroyed or damaged, as had 90 per cent of the oil storage tanks near Vinh. It remained to produce a post-facto 'justification' for the damage. The Congressional resolution (drafted, as we have seen, by the administration) approved and supported the determination of the President to 'take all necessary measures to repel any armed attack against the forces of the United States and to prevent further aggression'. It went on to declare that the US regarded international peace and security in Southeast Asia as vital to its national interest. Therefore the USA was prepared 'as the President determines', to take any action 'including the use of armed force, to assist any member or protocol state of the Southeast Asia Collective Defense Treaty requiring assistance in defense of its freedom'.[22] McNamara and Rusk testified on behalf of the resolution in secret sessions of the Senate and House of Representatives Foreign Relations Committee on 6 August. On the following day it was passed in the Senate by 88 votes to 2 and in the House by 416 to 0.

As the voting figures indicate, there were few Americans who questioned their government's policy at that time. Senator Wayne Morse, one of the two dissentients, did indeed beg Fulbright, the chairman of the Senate Foreign Relations Committee, to hold genuine hearings on the resolution and warned that its wording was too general and too open-ended for any president, especially President Johnson.[23] Subsequently it became clear that Morse and Gruening, the other opposer, were totally justified in their opposition. The US government had, it emerged, played a gigantic confidence trick on Congress and the American people.

In the first place it was exceedingly doubtful whether there had been any attack on 4 August. Captain John Herrick, commander of the Tonkin Gulf patrol, had signalled to the Pentagon: 'Review of action makes reported contacts and torpedoes fired appear doubtful. Freak weather reports and over-eager sonar men may have accounted for many reports. No actual sightings by *Maddox*. Suggest complete evaluation before further action.' Senator Fulbright, who was responsible for piloting the resolution through the Senate Foreign Relations Committee, later commented about Herrick's report: 'If I had known of that one telegram, if that had been put before me . . . I certainly don't think I would have rushed into action.'[24] Although they knew that visibility was bad ('blacker than the hubs of Hell') and that no US ship had sustained any damage, the Pentagon, after a perfunctory inquiry into Herrick's doubts, decided that there had been an attack by the North Vietnamese. Some months later, however, President Johnson, commenting on the Tonkin incident, remarked with a grin: 'For all I know, our Navy was shooting at whales out there.'[25]

Whether or not there had been an attack, the retaliatory air strikes could hardly be justified since there had been so much provocation of the North. While the 34A attacks had been generally ineffectual, they had given the enemy good reason for launching retaliatory strikes of their own. Herrick, having intercepted North Vietnamese radio traffic, realized that the enemy considered his destroyer patrol to be part of the operation that had attacked North Vietnamese installations on 31 July. When the *Maddox* was ordered, on 3 August, to return to the Gulf he warned that the continuance of the patrol was 'an unacceptable risk'.[26] It was undoubtedly an additional provocation. At the secret hearings on 6 August Morse questioned McNamara about the 34A raids and the connection between them and the destroyer patrol. McNamara lied to the senators, claiming that the US Navy had been unaware of any South Vietnamese actions and that the *Maddox* had been simply carrying out a routine patrol 'of the type we carry out all over the world at all times'.[27] Quite unscrupulously the Johnson administration turned the truth on its head, alleging that the US had been provoked by North Vietnam. Faced with such 'provocation' they beat the patriotic drum and almost all Americans fell in behind the flag. Eventually a price was paid for such sharp practice – widespread disillusionment. Fulbright, for example, was to comment later: 'I regret it more than anything I have ever done in my life, that I was the vehicle which took the resolution to the floor.'[28]

The Johnson administration was not the first to hoodwink Congress and the people, nor was it the last. Covert operations had been a feature of Kennedy's government: the Watergate affair has revealed some of the manipulations of the Nixon era. Even so, the Tonkin Gulf affair is worth particular attention. It was in the short-run so successful – a prime example of how the executive branch could manipulate the legislature and public opinion. The pattern was set for the rest of Johnson's term of office. The insiders simply assumed that they knew best; they would protect the people simultaneously from 'communism' and the truth. Hence the devious launching of the air-war, the build-up of ground troops, the covert operations against Laos, the undermining of any attempts to negotiate a settlement and so on and so on. Yet while they were diddling others, they were also deluding themselves. The Tonkin events left the President and his lieutenants with the illusion that they knew how to deal with North Vietnam.[29] They convinced themselves that they could achieve results by force, the use of which they could carefully regulate. In fact what they produced in August was a temporary success which involved the USA even more deeply in a war which was soon to get completely out of control. They managed to fool everyone except the enemy.

On the domestic front, it is true, Johnson continued to fool most of the people long enough to win handsomely in the elections. Between August and November he played alternately Dr Jekyll and Mr Hyde. In public he opposed widening the conflict and so being forced to send American boys to a war that 'ought to be fought by the boys of Asia'.[30] Less than two weeks after voicing those sentiments he approved preparations for extending the war in Laos. At the same time he indicated his readiness to take 'larger decisions' when necessary. The Pentagon analyst considered that by September there was a consensus in the government that 'overt military operations' against North Vietnam would begin in the new year.[31]

The Vietcong provided an occasion for one larger decision on 1 November, two days before the Presidential election. In a mortar attack on Bienhoa, an airfield near Saigon, they killed four Americans, destroyed five B-57 bombers and damaged eight others. The 'provocation' was greater than during the Tonkin Gulf incident and the Joint Chiefs favoured 'a prompt and strong response'.[32] Johnson decided to do nothing and his caution was well rewarded when on 3 November he gained his desired landslide victory over Goldwater.

With victory on the home front achieved the President was able to expedite preparations for an enlarged war. At the beginning of December he approved a two-phase bombing plan. Phase 1 involved 'reprisal' air-strikes and intensifying unpublicized attacks against the enemy. It was to be followed by Phase 2 – a sustained air-war against North Vietnam. On 10 December the Prime Minister of Laos agreed to US air-strikes against part of the Ho Chi Minh Trail, one of the supply lines between North and South Vietnam which ran through Laos. Such attacks, code-named Operation Barrell Roll, were part of Phase 1. There was to be no statement about the use of American planes unless one were lost. In that case the administration would claim that US aircraft were escorting reconnaissance flights 'as requested by the Laotian government'.[33] In January 1965, after the loss of two US jets, information about air operations in Laos began to filter through the security screen. Senator Morse, one of a small minority which took seriously press speculation that the US might be preparing to strike the North, condemned the air activity that had been taking place over Laos since 1964. The rule of law, he stated, had been replaced by the jungle law of military might. He predicted that unless US policy towards Southeast Asia changed there would be no hope of avoiding 'a massive war in Asia'.[34] As with the Tonkin resolution, Morse was later proved right. At the time he was ignored and the only change in American policy was to carry out the long-threatened bombing of North Vietnam.

It was finally precipitated by a mortar attack on 6 February against a United States contingent at Pleiku in which nine Americans were killed and seventy-six wounded. Within fourteen hours 49 US Navy jets had loosed their bombs and rockets on the North Vietnamese base at Donghoi. After a further Vietcong attack on an American barracks at Quinhon, Johnson ordered a second, heavier, reprisal raid on 11 February. Two days later he decided to launch Operation Rolling Thunder – the sustained air-war against North Vietnam.[35]

The consequences of US bombing in Indochina are examined in some detail in the next chapter. Here we might note briefly that there were many civilian casualties in the North, despite American claims that military targets could be destroyed with minimum loss of civilian life. Such casualties had exactly the opposite effect of that intended by Johnson's generals. They had urged bombing the North to coerce Ho's government to stop helping the insurgents in the South. In fact, however, Operation Rolling Thunder sharpened the spirit of resistance. James Cameron has pointed out that, 'From the moment the United States dropped its first bomb on the North of Vietnam, she welded the nation together unshakeably. Every bomb since was a bonus for Ho Chi Minh.'[36] Equally ineffective was the attempt to disrupt the economy. It was, as Cameron again noted, an immensely resilient peasant society, not easily wrecked by high-explosives. 'Every single industrial enterprise in the country could be ruined – and it would directly effect about 5 percent of the working population.'[37]

At the same time as it began its highly publicized attacks on the North, the US also launched an intensive air-war in South Vietnam. We consider later its full impact; it is appropriate at this point to observe that it was even more destructive than the bombing north of the seventeenth parallel. To the south of the line the US Air Force accomplished wholesale destruction of the land and its peasant population. By forcing millions of peasants to seek the safety of refugee camps – despite their appalling living conditions – the Americans did hurt the enemy. In a guerrilla war the peasants are the sea and the guerrillas the fish; if the sea can be dried up the fish die. On the other hand, the devastation increased hostility to the United States and their South Vietnamese allies. During the first year of bombing in the South Vietcong recruitment tripled.[38]

Even when the bombing was intensified enemy morale stayed high. Between 1965 and 1969 both North and South Vietnam were subjected to an incredible bombardment from the air. In that time about 4.5 million tons were dropped – 'over 70 tons of bombs for every square mile of Vietnam, North and South . . . about 500 pounds of bombs for every man, woman and child in Vietnam'.[39] Even that staggering demonstration of the US capacity for destruction was not enough to bring Johnson his victory.

The unlikelihood of the bombers delivering a crushing blow was appreciated early in the campaign. Indeed the air-war had scarcely begun before the military, realizing that it would produce no quick solution, were pressing for more ground troops in Vietnam. On 8 March 3,500 marines disembarked at Danang to protect its air base. At the end of the month the US Commander-in-Chief, Westmoreland, advised that the South Vietnamese army needed American reinforcements to 'hold the line'. On 1 April Johnson, so adamant a few months earlier about 'Asian boys' doing their own fighting, decided to use American ground troops for

'It says: "Sorry, but programming omitted factor of human spirit."'

14.

offensive action in South Vietnam. It was a drastic departure from previous policy and meant American involvement in another major land war in Asia. The President characteristically attempted to conceal the change from the public and it was not until 8 June that it 'crept out almost by accident in a State Department release . . .'[40] He was equally secretive when he announced on 28 July his decision to increase the number of US troops from 75,000 to 125,000. The fact was that he had decided that the American troop level in Vietnam would be 175,000 as a minimum and might reach the figure of 200,000. Thus the President carried out a major escalation of the war and, at the same time, a major deception on the American people. (Halberstam suggests that this point was the real beginning of the credibility gap.[41]) At the end of 1965 US forces in Vietnam numbered 184,000.[42]

The escalation and the deception continued in subsequent years. In February 1966, by which time the troops' total was 235,000, Johnson announced: 'We do not have on my desk at the moment any unfilled requests from General Westmoreland.'[43] In fact, Westmoreland had demanded, at the end of January, a total of 459,000. By September 1966 he had 325,000 of them; however he estimated that for 1967 he would require 542,500. In August 1967 Johnson agreed to a total of 525,000. Following the enemy's Tet offensive of February 1968 Westmoreland argued for a further

200,000 men to raise the total to more than 700,000. Thereupon Johnson finally called a halt: at the end of March he rebuffed his generals with a 'token' increase of some 20,000 men. Three years after launching his bombers and his battalions he recognized that victory had eluded him.

The American commander during those years, General Westmoreland, was an orthodox career soldier – 'his background was conventional war, and both his instincts and responses were conventional'.[44] His policy at first was to establish firm bases, whence he could strike the enemy. During 1966 he used small mobile groups to attack Vietcong concentrations: a tactic thwarted by the enemy's superior intelligence service. As his numbers and material increased he built up large, superbly equipped, multi-divisional forces with elaborate air support. They carried out huge 'search and destroy' missions which killed many Vietnamese but failed to deliver a decisive blow against the Vietcong. The enemy soldiers they killed were quickly replaced; one official commented that they were fighting Vietnam's birth-rate.[45] General Depuy, Westmoreland's chief strategist, thought that the answer was 'more bombs, more shells, more napalm . . . till the other side cracks and gives up'.[46] It did neither. Despite all Westmoreland's efforts the Vietcong were able to mass enough forces to launch a major offensive which helped to convince Johnson that a military victory was not possible in Vietnam.

On 31 January 1968, the period of the New Year (Tet) in Vietnam, between 50,000 and 60,000 Vietcong, with the co-operation of hundreds of thousands of urban residents, occupied most of the populated areas in South Vietnam. Even the US Embassy in Saigon was captured and held for some 24 hours. Hué, the principal city in central Vietnam, was occupied until the offensive petered out, under devastating American bombardment, at the end of February. By that time the guerrillas had attacked 34 provincial centres, 64 district towns and most cities of any size. Attempts were made to play down the Tet offensive: the VC, it was claimed, had sustained crippling losses. From the Pentagon history, however, it is clear that the offensive had caught the US leaders unawares and that 'its strength, length and intensity prolonged this shock'.[47]

At the end of February Johnson ordered a complete review of American policy in Vietnam. Clark Clifford, soon to replace

McNamara as Secretary of Defense, convened a group of senior advisers which presented a memorandum in favour of curtailing the war. It contended that even if a further 200,000 troops were deployed, as Westmoreland wished, the US would still be unable to win the war. Hanoi, it argued, had enough reserves to match a further American commitment. Also, if the US continued to pour more and more resources into the war, it would become difficult to convince critics that they were not in fact destroying Vietnam in order to 'save' it from Communism. Such a continued diversion of resources would also accentuate the discontent of those who felt that urgent domestic problems were being neglected as a result of the war. There was a serious risk, warned Clifford's group, of provoking 'a domestic crisis of unprecedented proportions.'[48]

Despite the opposition of his generals, the President, as already noted, did check the flow of troops to Vietnam. In a crucial speech on 31 March he announced the 'token' increase of 20,000. At the same time he declared that further attacks on North Vietnam by US aircraft and Navy vessels would be limited to an area north of the demilitarized zone. Thus the area exempted from bombing contained nearly 90 per cent of the population and almost all the territory of the North. All the major populated centres were to be spared further attack.[49] At the end of his speech Johnson, having reduced the bombing 12,000 miles away, dropped a bombshell on Washington. He withdrew from the Presidential election of 1968.

We consider subsequently how public opinion turned against Johnson's handling of the war. It was recognition of their disillusionment that persuaded him to renounce his hope of re-election. After his withdrawal he was virtually powerless to make any conclusive move on Vietnam. He had to some degree limited the escalation of the war but did not have the political status, far less the personal inclination, to bring it to an end. On 3 April he announced that Hanoi was ready to meet US representatives to discuss the issues. Thereafter the war dragged on, as did the campaign to elect a new President. Johnson's war was virtually over: Nixon's was still to come.

Seven

THE DEVASTATION OF VIETNAM

It took some time for ordinary Americans to appreciate the impact of the US presence in Vietnam. They were told repeatedly by their leaders that their objective was the independence of South Vietnam. Shortly after the escalation in the spring of 1965 Johnson had explained that Americans wanted nothing for themselves. They would use their power with restraint not only to protect South Vietnam's freedom but also to help all countries of Southeast Asia. The task was nothing less than to 'enrich the hopes and existence of more than a hundred million people'.[1] Such stressing of America's constructive purpose in Vietnam was for a time highly functional. The administration was able to prosecute the war with the idealistic backing of most Americans. On the other hand, when the truth emerged, the shock was all the greater. The truth was that Indochina had been devastated by its *soi-disant* defenders.

In 1968, when the nature of the war had become apparent, one British observer wrote: 'America protects the freedom of the Vietnamese by helicopters armed with batteries of machine-guns, which spray entire villages with bullets and "flush out" – the clean, antiseptic military phrase – their inhabitants; by cumbersome, big-bellied aircraft which, every week, pour hundreds of tons of herbicides on growing crops. They drop steel-blades . . . by the thousand and clusters of steel balls, the size of hand grenades, which break on impact and scatter lethal pellets through the thin partitions of the peasants' huts. In Vietnam the treasures of the American way of death are spread out as in a shop-window.'[2]

The point has been very often made that the Americans sought to achieve 'liberation' by means of destruction. If we remember another equally obvious point, that the guerrillas were largely indistinguishable from the other peasants and lived among them, we can appreciate that the destruction of the Vietcong necessarily entailed the devastation of the villages and the death of the villagers. In the Vietnam war there were usually no conventional military fronts and no areas where guerrilla influence was wholly eradicated. From the American standpoint the front line was everywhere and everyone was potentially the enemy.

Those realities had determined the conduct of the conflict even before its intensification in 1965. Under Diem there had been a virtual war against the peasants. In December 1962 the State Department intelligence section noted that extensive use of artillery and aerial bombardment by the South Vietnamese government, in its attempts to eliminate the guerrillas, had 'killed many innocent peasants and made many others more willing than before to co-operate with the Viet Cong'.[3] Even in this early stage the casualties were appalling. The French authority, Bernard Fall, estimated that 89,000 Vietcong had been killed between 1961 and April 1965.[4] Given the indiscriminate bombardment of whole areas where there were no easily definable military targets, civilian casualties were generally very high.

Until 1965 South Vietnamese peasants had suffered largely at the hands of their 'own' air force.[5] From February of that year they had to contend also with the US Air Force. As already noted, it was then that the long-pondered decision to bomb the North was taken. In April, however, it was decided that, in the use of American air power, priority should be given to South Vietnam. By May large areas had been designated 'free bombing zones' where 'tens of thousands of tons of bombs, rockets, napalm and cannon fire' were poured in every week.[6] In June, Johnson authorized raids on South Vietnam by huge B-52 bombers with a standard load of fifty-one 750-pound bombs of high explosive or many more incendiary bombs. Operating from Guam or Thailand, they attacked from 30,000 to 40,000 feet, too high to be seen or heard. They blasted and burned large areas of jungle, roads, buildings, fields and, of course, people.[7] One American study found, not surprisingly, that B-52s were 'the most devastating and frightening weapons used so far against the VC'.[8] As the war persisted the bombing increased, from 315,000 tons in 1965 to 1,388,000 tons in 1969.[9]

Bombardment from the air was only one aspect of the 'unparalleled, lavish use of firepower as a substitute for manpower' which, according to a Pentagon official, was the main feature of American tactics in Vietnam.[10] Artillery bombardment was more frequent and may have been even more destructive. Ground ammunition expended increased from 577,000 tons in 1966 to 1,374,000 tons in 1969. In 1968 and 1969 the US was using about 7,700 to 7,800 tons of ground and air ordnance in an average day – about 500 times the quantity used by the NLF forces.[12] Those statistics indicate how the scale of war enlarged and say something about the great disparity of resources between the two sides. The extent of the destruction they represent can, however, scarcely be conceived. For any picture of it to emerge the figures must be supplemented with accounts of a land pock-marked with bomb craters, of charred fields, forests where trees could not be felled since they were full of shell fragments.[13] The successes of lavish firepower require to be measured in terms of fields, where rice once grew, being submerged in sea-water following the bombing of a dike; of the hills overlooking the flooded rice fields being 'ironed' – a term used by the peasants to indicate that they were riddled with bomb fragments, mines and unexploded artillery shells.[14] Another index of American technological achievement was that South Vietnam, which until 1964 was an exporter of rice, became, after 1965, a heavy rice importer.

Crop destruction was achieved not only by bombardment but also by chemical warfare. Defoliation of trees to facilitate the detection of guerrillas had been approved by Kennedy in 1962.[15] Known as Operation Ranch Hand, the programme was carried out by a group flying C-123 aircraft whose slogan was 'Only We Can Prevent Forests'.[16] The defoliation programme was supplemented by an anti-crop project and by the end of 1966 more than half the C-123 missions were targeted against crops.[17] In July 1966 the *New York Times* revealed that, since 1962, the spraying had blighted some 130,000 acres of rice and other food plants.[18] During the next few years chemical warfare expanded rapidly. In the first nine months of 1967 defoliants were sprayed on 843,606 acres and crop-killing chemicals on another 121,400 acres. The US Air Force estimated an expenditure of $70.8 million on destructive chemicals in the year 1968–9, an increase of $24.9 million over the previous year.[19] An American authority commented in May 1968 that, while the long-term effects of spraying were imponderable, the short-term results were certain: leaves, trees, rice plants and other vegetation were dead or dying: many insects, birds and animals and some human beings also had either migrated or died of starvation. The North Vietnamese were, he commented, fortunate – they had only bombs to contend with.[20]

The various methods of destruction employed by the US in Vietnam were very costly and took a good deal of organizing; there was nothing haphazard about them. Their purpose was, as the American authorities have acknowledged often enough, to eliminate the guerrillas. Since the guerrillas were embedded in the peasant society, their elimination involved the destruction of that society. It was not possible to undertake such a task without killing many innocent people. In practice that was what happened. Naturally enough US military spokesmen and apologists have tried to uphold the fiction that they did their best not to harm non-combatants. They have had an uphill struggle against a mountain of evidence that in Vietnam the indiscriminate killing of civilians was as American as cherry pie.

A few random examples may be cited. Charles Mohr, Saigon correspondent of the *New York Times*, reported on 5 September 1965: 'This is strategic bombing in a friendly, allied country. Since the Vietcong doctrine is to insulate themselves among the population and the population is powerless to prevent their presence, no one here seriously doubts that significant numbers of innocent civilians are dying every day in South Viet-Nam.'[21] Another *Times* reporter, Jack Langguth, commented on official attempts to cover up such facts. On one occasion the US authorities claimed that the victims of an air strike were Vietcong soldiers. Having investigated the incident Langguth discovered that 'three out of four patients seeking treatment in a Vietnamese hospital afterward for burns from napalm or jellied gasoline were village women'.[22] The military were not always so secretive. A Lieutenant-Colonel who introduced a French journalist, Jean Bertolino, to his immediate superior volunteered the information that the General hunted the Vietcong with a rifle from his Iroquois helicopter. The General shrugged off Bertolino's comment that surely it was not possible from the air to distinguish the Vietcong from civilians.[23]

Katsuichi Honda, a Japanese journalist, once found himself at the receiving end of helicopter fire: 'They seemed to fire whimsically . . . even though they were not being shot at from the ground nor could they identify the people as NLF. They did it impulsively for fun, using the farmers for targets as if in a hunting mood. They are hunting Asians.'[24] American soldiers have them-selves contributed to the evidence: a helicopter gunner has claimed that he was ordered to kill unarmed civilians; a medic has testified that some twenty-seven civilians at a peaceful meeting were killed by US tanks firing 'a barrage of tiny arrow-like nails'.[25] Many other examples could be quoted *ad nauseam*.

Orders involving attacks on civilians emanated from the very top. Neil Sheehan, compiler of the *New York Times* edition of the Pentagon Papers, has claimed that the 'highest level of authority in Saigon' vetoed a suggestion that the policy of unrestricted bombing and shelling should be reconsidered. The authority held fast to the idea of defeating the Vietnamese Communists 'by oblit-erating their strategic base, the rural population'.[26] We might note that from the Pentagon Papers it is clear that the President and his policy makers had no illusions about its consequences when they authorized the campaign against the rural society in South Vietnam.[27] Against such a background, the massacre at My Lai, which produced world-wide reactions of shock and horror, appears simply as one more incident in a saga of indiscriminate violence.[28]

Apart from causing wholesale devastation and innumerable casualties, the bombs, shells, napalm, chemicals, mines and so on were successful in 'generating' many refugees. That was the euphemism for uprooting millions of peasants from their villages and penning them in camps where they could no longer give support to the NLF. The forced evacuation of the peasantry caused problems for the guerrillas but was not sufficient to eliminate them. It did however cause great misery. There is no accurate figure for the refugees 'generated' during Johnson's war: estimates vary from two million to four million. In any case they were a substantial proportion of the whole population. Their living conditions were exceedingly bad. Mary McCarthy, the novelist, visited one camp where a stagnant duck-pond provided the only water for 700 people to drink, wash and cook. Another duck-pond, slightly larger, supplied the remaining 800 inhabitants. 'There were,' she noted, 'no sanitary facilities of any kind; we saw women and children squatting; garbage was strewn in front of the huts, which had earth floors and inflammable old straw roofing.'[29] Senator Edward Kennedy inspected some camps where thousands of people were 'literally starving to death'. He revealed that the annual

15. President Nguyen Van Thieu.

expenditure on the refugee programme was less than the amount spent by the US on the war in half a day.[30]

The refugee situation, like every other problem, was completely mishandled by the South Vietnamese government. Ostensibly – we may recall – the US aspired to ensure that the people of South Vietnam had an efficient and democratic government. In fact it was neither. Between 1964 and 1967 the military hierarchy played musical chairs for the political leadership of the country. In 1964 Nguyen Khanh staged a coup against Diem's successors. He himself was 'neurotic, paranoiac, disliked by both older officers and younger officers, and like his predecessors, totally overwhelmed by the political problems he faced'.[31] Of the numerous other figures who emerged to succeed him we might mention the two most prominent. Nguyen Cao Ky, a young adventurer whose hero was, he proudly proclaimed, Adolf Hitler, was Prime Minister from 1965 to 1967. In that year he was relegated to the post of Vice-President by his rival Nguyen Van Thieu who became President. Thieu was to provide stability of a kind in that he managed to keep himself in power. His regime had the durability of Diem's. Also like Diem's, and every other South Vietnamese government, it was corrupt, repressive, totally dependent on US support and ineffectual in dealing with the major problems of a society convulsed by a devastating war.

Instances abound of peculation and malversation in South Vietnamese governments.[32] Fitzgerald has described how in 1966 Ky and Thieu made the arrangements necessary to support 'a new and more stable system of corruption'. The generals commanding the First and Second Corps were allowed to enrich themselves through military preferments and disposing of US commodities; the Fourth Corps commander traded in rice and opium; the Defence Minister flourished by means of property deals. Thieu put his financial transactions into the efficient, diamond-bedecked hands of his wife. Ky – more concerned with power than mere personal enrichment – used the money that came his way to buy provincial officials and to hire his own band of thugs.[33] One of the most serious forms of corruption, in an allegedly democratic country, is the rigging of elections. The evidence suggests that every election in South Vietnam has been rigged. Having examined the 1967 election, for example, Lederer concluded that the Thieu–Ky regime was not backed by the people; that it had to resort to bribery, terror and disqualification of unfriendly voters to stay in power. He considered that the regime was 'afraid of the democratic process'.[34]

Fearing the democratic process, the cliques who have governed South Vietnam have simply avoided it. After the fall of Diem even official Washington admitted how repressive his regime had been. Similar repression continued after 1963 and was constantly condoned by the United States. In September 1968, Professor Ly Chanh Trung, a prominent South Vietnamese Catholic intellectual, declared: '. . . the inhabitants of the southern part of Viet Nam have not been able to enjoy freedom, and have not had the chance to be masters of their own destiny, precisely because the Americans, in the name of the protectors of freedom, have, in fact, been protecting regimes which stamp out that freedom.'[35] The successors of Diem have used his methods: suppression of newspapers; banning opposition groups; maintaining camps for political prisoners – and so on. A limitation of political freedom is specifically included in the 1967 constitution, of which Article V states: 'The Republic of Viet-Nam opposes communism in every form. Every activity designed to propagandize or carry out communism is prohibited.'[36] Non-communist opponents of the military juntas appreciated that communism was a category that could be extended to include, for example, Buddhists.[37]

Like Diem, the generals used the apparatus of oppression and rigged elections principally in order to stay where they were. The ultimate corruption of the Saigon regimes was their complete egocentrism. Their corruption was not a falling away from an ideal, since they had no ideals; even their anti-communism was a dogma of convenience, a key to America's treasure-chest. While even Diem had possessed some shreds of national consciousness,

'If there's an election tomorrow, which general would you vote for?'

16. Cartoon, 1966, comments on the army's domination of South Vietnam's disturbed politics.

his successors had no nationalist credentials whatsoever. With one exception, every South Vietnamese officer above the rank of lieutenant-colonel (in 1967) had served with the French army against the Vietminh nationalists.[38] Khanh, expelled from the Vietminh for 'tiredness' and lack of discipline, eventually became an officer in the élite gardes mobiles. Ky joined the French when he came of age and trained in France as a bomber pilot. Thieu served against the Vietminh for the duration of the first Indochina War. As Fitzgerald observes, they did not see the war as a national political struggle but 'as an unlooked-for boost to their otherwise unpromising careers'.[39]

Under the Americans they entered into their tawdry inheritance. They were part of the gimcrack élite that enriched itself through contact with the new imperial power. Together with the hotel owners, the licensed importers, the real-estate dealers and the brothel-keepers, they were the people who profited from the war.[40] Thus they were not concerned about the damage that was done to the economy by the huge American military presence. With their connections they need not worry that, by a conservative estimate, the cost of living in the cities rose by 170 per cent between January 1965 and the end of 1967 and that the price of rice, the staple diet, increased 200 per cent. Insouciantly they encouraged the debasement of Vietnamese society, such as an American journalist observed in 1966: 'A drive through Saigon demonstrates another fashion in which the social system works. Virtually all the new construction consists of luxury appartments and office buildings financed by Chinese business-men of affluent Vietnamese with relations or connexions with the régime. The buildings are destined to be rented to Americans. Saigon's workers live, as they always have, in fetid slums on the city's outskirts . . . Bars and bordellos, thousands of young Vietnamese women degrading themselves as bar girls and prostitutes, gangs of hoodlums and beggars and children selling their older sisters and picking pockets have become ubiquitous features of urban life.'[41]

A leadership which actively co-operated with a foreign power whose presence not only corrupted the cities but was also destroying the very fabric of life in the countryside was hardly likely to be popular. With US support and by strong-arm methods the generals held firmly to the fruits of office. While they did so the NLF emerged as the only widely based, though illegal, political movement in South Vietnam. We have seen that, under Diem, the NLF had organized an effective opposition to his regime. In the chaotic situation following his death the NLF strengthened its hold on the countryside. By 1965 it was poised to seize power – hence the massive American intervention. Within five years of being set-up the NLF had created 'a government and an army out of the disordered and intractable society of South Vietnam'.[42] The Front succeeded because it filled the gap created by Saigon regimes whose interests were at odds with the needs of the people and because it was superbly organized.

Responsibility for ensuring 'correct' attitudes and efficient organization was in the hands of cadres drawn from the People's Revolutionary Party. Founded in 1962, it was the Communist Party of South Vietnam and formed the inner core of the NLF. According to one of its own directives it was like a plant and the people were the soil that nourished it.[43] The cadres, after living with the peasants, gradually reorganized the patterns of their daily lives. As they developed personal ties with the villagers they encouraged them to establish village organizations. The most important were the Farmers Associations which decided land disputes, assessed taxes on rice crops, planned irrigation works and organized the defences of the village. Other associations regulated the work of the women and the youth. Everyone participated in village defence through membership of the militia and, in many villages, by making uniforms, weapons and medicines. Given sufficient time, the cadres stimulated the peasants to turn their villages into agricultural co-operatives and military bases. An established Front village might also provide a school, its own newspaper and dispensary and would, in addition, be a training camp for new revolutionaries.

Such remarkable changes were the result of the centralized direction of the PRP, together with the dedication and patience of the cadres. Their patient approach to the peasants contrasted with the generally arrogant and peremptory behaviour of the government officials. One explanation of that contrast is that while the government forces derived their strength from American largesse, the Front depended for its existence on the support of the peasantry. The cadres made a point of stressing their dependence which in fact encouraged the villagers to give their assistance. For many peasants it was a novel and pleasant experience to feel that others depended on them. Such an attitude contributed to a sense of community and allowed the individual villagers to feel that their efforts did have real significance. Commentators on the Front have often undervalued the popular and voluntary element in its organizational success. The Front certainly used strong-arm tactics and in cold-blood killed government officials to strengthen its own position. Generally, however, it succeeded through persuasion rather than by naked violence.

The thoroughness of the NLF was shown in the training it gave its troops. Cadres began by ensuring that the recruits had the right attitude. They destroyed, for example, the political passivity characteristic of so many peasants by inculcating hatred of the enemy. They appreciated that hatred was 'the key to the vast, secret torrents of energy that lay buried within the Vietnamese people . . .'[44] Only when they had learned to discipline that hatred, to use it 'creatively' were the recruits entrusted with weapons. Politics was paramount. Military training was, however, painstakingly thorough. Attacks on an enemy position might be rehearsed over and over again before the real thing. Morale was kept high by ensuring, for example, that every soldier knew precisely what his role was and why it was important. Self-criticism meetings ensured that mistakes were corrected and also kept lines of communication in the army open to a remarkable degree.

The political and military achievements of the NLF at first owed little to their friends in North Vietnam. From 1959 onwards, it is true, many volunteers, mostly of southern origin, infiltrated south to join the Front. In addition the North Vietnamese provided some armaments by way of the Ho Chi Minh trail. However, Northern participation in the war was marginal until the very success of the largely independent NLF forces precipitated the US bombing of North Vietnam.[45] Thereafter the North Vietnamese became increasingly involved. Despite the US bombing the Hanoi government was able to send support to the NLF and to reinforce them with their own troops. When the Americans launched their offensive there were only some 400 North Vietnamese regulars in the south. By December 1965 there were 14,000; at the end of 1967 the number was 55,000. The bulk of the fighting in the south was still being done by the various groups under the NLF – some 240,000 of them.[46] More and more, however, the southerners were dependent on the North. Meanwhile the North was being obliged to wage its own war against the US Air Force.

The American leaders maintained, as usual, that they were bombing military targets only in the North. However, eye-witness reports of damage to non-military targets, such as hospitals, and accounts of civilian casualties were so numerous and from such reliable sources that the official version was quickly discredited.[47] Even according to a CIA estimate, by 1966, after 161,000 tons of bombs had fallen, there had been almost 30,000 civilian casualties.[48] While the casualties continued to mount, they did not have the effect desired by the Johnson administration. In October 1966 McNamara informed the President that popular morale in the

17. One-man air-raid shelters in Hanoi.

North had not been significantly weakened by the air strikes. He noted, furthermore, that North Vietnam had been able to improvise transportation and that, 'because of the primitive nature of their economy', Rolling Thunder would affect only a small fraction of the people. There was 'very little hope' that Ho Chi Minh would lose control of the population. Confident of popular support, the government was vigorously prosecuting the war. McNamara's memorandum pointed out that, despite difficulties created by the bombs, the communists had actually increased the southward flow of supplies and manpower. Hanoi's determination to support the 'insurgency' was as firm as ever.[49]

Neither Johnson nor the Joint Chiefs were convinced by McNamara's argument in favour of 'stabilizing' Rolling Thunder. The pressure on the North was maintained and then increased. The so-called 'pauses' in the bombing were public relations exercises, intended to deceive the American public, not in fact to de-escalate. In 1967 US planes mined rivers in the North and bombed industrial targets near Hanoi. During the same year the air-war in Laos was also secretly intensified.[50] Still it remained ineffectual. McConnell, Air Force Chief of Staff, was moved to complain that he had 'never been so goddam frustrated'. Morale in North Vietnam, despite the terrible destruction, maiming and loss of life remained high.

The whole nation had been mobilized for the war effort. Children and older people were evacuated from the more obvious targets. Those who remained re-arranged their daily lives. Movement of supplies, for example, took place at night when targets were more difficult to identify. Important materials were dispersed to make them harder to hit. Ingenious means were devised for repairing quickly the roads, railways and bridges that were repeatedly bombed and promptly made viable again. As much as possible was carried on bicycles – a primitive but effective and almost invulnerable form of transport. Armed with MIG fighters and Soviet SAM, surface-to-air missiles, the defence forces accounted for some 1,400 US aircraft between 1965 and 1968.

Together the NLF and the North Vietnamese refused to yield even after enduring a bloody mauling from the world's greatest military power. After three terrible years it was not they who cracked but Lyndon Johnson. The war ended his career and had also the most profound effect on the whole of the United States.

Eight

THE EFFECT OF THE WAR ON THE UNITED STATES

During the period between the two Presidential elections of 1964 and 1968 the war in Vietnam became the major issue in the political life of the United States. Few people in 1964 could have imagined that, within four years, the war would deny Johnson the chance of re-election. The voters who thought they had given a landslide victory to the peace candidate naturally expected US involvement to remain at a low level. Johnson was, however, as we have seen, preparing to deepen that involvement. Appreciating the lack of enthusiasm in Congress and among the public for such a move, he escalated the war by stealth. In doing so he assumed that America's military might would soon defeat the NLF and its allies from North Vietnam, which he once contemptuously dismissed as a 'raggedy-ass little fourth-rate country'.[1] There would be protests from those he regarded as 'extreme' liberals but he expected that most Americans would quickly accept a *fait accompli*. South Vietnam would be secure and in the USA Johnson would, through a programme of social reform, create the Great Society.

One of his reasons for taking a hard line on the war was to protect himself against right-wingers who might oppose his reform legislation. 'If I don't go in now,' he said, 'and they show later I should have gone, then they'll be all over me in Congress. They won't be talking about my civil rights bill, or education or beautification [of the environment]. No sir, they'll push Vietnam up my ass every time. Vietnam. Vietnam. Vietnam. Right up my ass.'[2] Having 'gone in' his right flank, so to speak, was secure. Since the intervention would be over quickly, the left-wing opposition would, he calculated, soon fizzle out.

The 'success' of another military venture in April 1965 suggested that a show of force in Vietnam might be equally effective. Claiming that a revolution, which in fact was attempting to remove an unpopular dictator, was a communist plot, Johnson despatched 23,000 US marines to the Dominican Republic. The revolution was quickly crushed and American interests preserved. Critics complained about his high-handed action but he ignored them and the incident made little impact on the mass of the people. Johnson's intention was to dispose of the Vietnam problem in the same uncompromising way.[3]

There was a certain plausibility about his approach. Americans had in the past accepted an intemperate use of force by their governments, with only a minority, as in the Dominican affair, affected by scruples of conscience. Furthermore, the disparity in resources between the US and its opponents was likely to ensure rapid results. Such calculations, however, did not take account of the enemy's tenacity. Under the most concentrated assault the Vietnamese remained defiant. As the war dragged on the US victory stayed elusive, opposition to it grew. By prolonging the conflict the Vietnamese forced the American people to consider what it was doing to their own society and to ask what kind of society it was that could get involved in such a war. During the whole of the Cold War period conformity had been an American virtue. Loyalty oaths, congressional investigations, emphasis on the state ideology in schools, manipulation of public opinion by the media – all had conditioned Americans to feel that the questioning of their institutions was unpatriotic. The Vietnam War, however, was called into question, particularly by young Americans. Once the questioning began it did not stop at the war which, after all, was only a product of the society as a whole.

Charles Reich in *The Greening of America* commented that: '. . . the war seemed to sum up the evils of our society: destruction of people, destruction of environment, depersonalized use of technology, war by the rich and powerful against the poor and helpless, justification based on abstract rationality, hypocrisy and lies, and a demand that the individual, regardless of his conscience, values or self, make himself into a part of the war machine, an impersonal projectile bringing death to other people.'[4] Only a minority of Americans were moved to such radical criticism. However, in a country so populous as the United States even a minority could be substantial and included among the critics were men of some influence. Senator Fulbright, for example, chairman of the Senate Foreign Relations Committee, was, like Reich,

18. **Young Americans in an anti-war protest.**

critical of the power in the USA of the military-industrial complex.

In his Farewell Address to the Nation in 1961 President Eisenhower had sounded a warning to his fellow Americans. 'In the councils of Government,' he said, 'we must guard against the acquisition of unwarranted influence . . . by the military-industrial complex. The potential for the disastrous rise of misplaced power exists and will persist. We must never let the weight of this combination endanger our liberties or democratic processes.'[5] His warning went largely unheeded. Nearly seven years later Fulbright pointed out that a large sector of the economy was dependent on so-called 'defence' expenditure. The industries and businesses supplying military needs were, he said, the largest producers of goods and services in the United States. During the fiscal year 1968–9 they would 'pour some $45 billion into over 5,000 cities and towns where over 8 million Americans, counting members of the Armed Forces . . . approximately 10 percent of the labor force, would earn their living from defense spending'.[6] The generals, industrialists and businessmen who manipulated such vast expenditures inevitably constituted a major political force. Together with the politicians, workers, writers and advertising men involved with them, they were a powerful group concerned to perpetuate foreign military commitments, to introduce and expand new weapons systems and so ensure, in Fulbright's words, 'the militarization of large segments of our national life'.[7] Unlike other groups, the military-industrial complex was so enormous that there was no effective counterweight to it.

The longer the Vietnam War lasted the more people began to appreciate just how powerful it had become and to realize the consequences of having so much power concentrated in such hands. The war did not create the military-industrial complex; it did, however, emphasize its influence and prompted its critics to speak out – even if rather belatedly. An editorial in the *New York Times* of 1 September 1967, for example, voiced its concern about the power of the Pentagon. It claimed that the inability of the Congress to uncover the truth (by then widely suspected) about the Tonkin Gulf incident had 'underscored the erosion in the constitutional requirement for legislative control over the war making power'.[8] There no longer existed in fact the constitutional balance that, in theory, kept the military power under civilian control.

The Times was commenting publicly on a state of affairs that was well known to insiders in the political world – that there was a division of opinion between the Secretary of Defense, McNamara, and the military hierarchy. By the autumn of 1967 McNamara was sceptical about military victory. Nevertheless the generals continued to argue that if they were given the tools – specifically more troops – they could finish the job. In such a situation only the President had the authority to 'restore civilian control of national policy'. At that juncture, however, he was desperately hoping that the war was still winnable. He felt that McNamara had 'gone dovish' on him and in November decided to remove him from office.[9] His removal did nothing to allay criticism from other quarters. Senator Thurston Morton of Kentucky, for example, attacked Johnson for allowing himself to be brainwashed by the military-industrial complex into believing that there could still be a military solution in Vietnam.[10]

Congressmen had good reason to feel that their own power had been usurped. The most glaring example of that usurpation was that the war was being fought without the constitutional requirements being fulfilled. According to the Constitution, Congress alone has the power to declare war. It had not, however, legitimized hostilities against North Vietnam, although the executive had chosen to regard the Tonkin Gulf resolution as a functional declaration of war.[11] When we reflect on how that resolution was passed it is clear (and was by 1967 obvious to many Congressmen) that the elected representatives of the people had been manipulated by the President and his advisers. The fact that Americans were killing and being killed in an undeclared war indicated that the constitutional processes had lost some of their validity.[12] It was all the more ominous that, while more and more representatives were objecting to the situation, many were prepared to accept it. Congress continued to vote the money necessary to pursue policies which were in large measure determined by the Pentagon. Congressmen were ready to condemn critics of the war for their 'sense of utter irresponsibility' while they themselves allowed the executive and the military establishment to go beyond their legal authority. Although many were roused to protest against the conduct of the war, the majority were willing to rubber-stamp decisions made by unelected, unrepresentative élites.[13] However, as the results of those decisions became known the dissentient voices increased inside and outside the Congress.

Perhaps the most tragic consequence for Americans were the war casualties. Despite the strategy of replacing manpower with firepower and despite a highly efficient provision of medical services in the combat zones, US casualties multiplied as the war continued. Less than 2,000 Americans were killed in Vietnam in 1965. In 1966 the figure was 5,000 and in 1968 it was 14,000. By the end of 1967 the dead and wounded exceeded 100,000.[14] As the coffins and the maimed veterans returned home many people who had loyally waved the flag began to wonder whether President Thieu and his regime were after all worth such sacrifices.

Though significant, the casualty figures directly affected a small percentage of the total population. On the other hand, the material, as opposed to the human, cost of the war affected all Americans in some measure. With full-scale US intervention in Vietnam there had been a dramatic increase, from $105 million to more than $2,000 million per month.[15] Characteristically, the Johnson administration attempted to conceal the true cost, claiming that it was some $800 million per month. To admit the true figure might, Johnson felt, threaten his Great Society legislation. While Congress might be persuaded to finance either an expensive war or the social reforms he desired, it was unlikely to underwrite both. The President did not doubt that the reforms would be sacrificed first. He therefore lied about the military expenditure. The Council of Economic Advisers, increasingly sceptical about the government's statistics, demanded more exact estimates and urged a tax increase to meet some of the cost. Fearing that it might give the game away, Johnson delayed his request for an increase in taxes and so helped to create an inflation whose political impact became 'almost as serious a political issue in 1968 as the war itself'.[16] The President eventually suggested an income tax surcharge in his budget message of January 1967 – a proposal which was not agreed by Congress until the summer of 1968, by which time the inflation was 'full-blown' and was provoking a great deal of anti-war sentiment.

The sheer scale of expenditure (which could not be concealed for ever) also created doubts. Was it possible, even with the enormous resources of the USA, to devote nearly $30,000 million every year to the Vietnam War? Was it necessary to spend so much to defeat a nation of backward peasants? Senator Hartke threw some light on that question in a magazine article about a huge amphibious operation in the Mekong Delta, to which US taxpayers contributed $16 million. Since a total of 21 Vietcong were killed, the cost of a single enemy death was no less than $800,000.[17] Another senator commented on the anomaly of spending $66 million per day 'trying to save the 16 million people of South Vietnam while leaving the plight of 20 million urban poor [in the USA] unresolved'.[18] (The South Vietnamese might have doubted whether the bombs, napalm and so on paid for by the $66 million were indeed intended to 'save' them.) A similar point was made by a prominent retired general, Gavin, who early in 1967 recommended, in testimony before the Senate Foreign

Relations Committee, ending the conflict as quickly and as reasonably as possible. He later remarked that America's domestic programmes were 'grossly underfunded, especially in the poverty area . . . as a consequence of the Vietnam war'.[19]

Such criticisms helped to intensify opposition to the war, particularly when riots by black Americans in 1965 and 1967 seemed to confirm the thesis that the enormous cost of the war was inhibiting much needed social reform. That specific point demands some further consideration. While the Vietnamese imbroglio undoubtedly had an important impact on the racial question, its effect was not to be measured simply in terms of finance.

President Johnson had made a brave attempt to tackle the racial issue, perhaps the most intractable of America's social problems. The passing of the Civil Rights Act of 1964 and the Voting Rights Act of 1965 sought to fulfil some of the promises made to black Americans a hundred years previously. It was soon clear, however, that they were by no means satisfied by such belated guarantees of their rights as citizens. In August 1965, the very month in which the Voting Rights Act was passed, they rioted for a week in Los Angeles. Thirty-four people died, over a thousand were injured and some six hundred buildings were destroyed or seriously damaged. Two years later there were even more serious disturbances in over sixty cities across the United States, particularly in Newark and Detroit. In July 1967, more than a thousand black militants from all over America attended a Black Power conference. Their leaders asserted their right to control their own destiny, demanding not extra handouts from the Federal Government but an end to the exploitative system that had kept them a subject race. They condemned the war in Vietnam not simply because it diverted dollars away from the black ghettos but because it was a foreign parallel to the subjection of the blacks in the USA. They compared themselves with the Vietnamese: both were, in their view, victims of a racist white government, prepared to use violence to protect its power at home and abroad.

That point had been made in 1965 by a former president of Students for a Democratic Society who alleged that the murders in Vietnam were similar to the murders of blacks in the American South. The refusal to deal with the needs and aspirations of people in Vietnam was, he said, the same as the refusal to deal with the problems of millions of poor people in the USA. What kind of system was it, he enquired, that allowed the US or any other country to 'seize the destinies of other people and use them callously for their own ends'?[20] Both militant black Americans and radical young white Americans attacked 'the system' in the USA. The manifesto of a conference attended by both groups in 1967 declared that whoever was running America, it was not the American people. Delegates went on to promise an end to the devastation of Vietnam and the destruction of other countries by the 'economic and political pressures of the great powers . . .'[21] In the event, advocates of Black Power were unwilling to co-operate with the whites and the two movements went their separate ways. Both, however, remained united in their condemnation of the Vietnam War, the most outrageous product of a system which they both reviled.

Radical young Americans discovered a number of ways to express their opposition to the war and the system. They campaigned against conscription by publicly burning their draft cards and refusing to be inducted into the armed services. They attacked the system of selective service which, by deferring military service for those who had gained certain academic qualifications, ensured that many more of the poor than of the middle and upper-income groups were called up. Files in draft centres were destroyed and some of those who were academically qualified refused to take the tests which could have guaranteed them deferment. Troop trains were delayed by people sitting on the railway lines. Other forms of sit-ins were held in university campuses. Teach-ins were also organized to counteract the official version of the war. Underground newspapers were published and underground organizations emerged to help draft resisters to avoid jail by fleeing abroad. Mass demonstrations were held at which the resisters came into violent conflict with the police and national guardsmen.

In October 1967 tens of thousands of mainly young people participated in a mass peace demonstration in Washington, culminating in a march on the Pentagon building. Johnson subsequently praised the soldiers and police for their outstanding performance in containing 'violence and lawlessness'.[22] His opinion echoed those of millions of Americans who considered the opponents of the war as no better than traitors. Even so the active critics did prevent the powerful state propaganda apparatus from going unchallenged; their campaigns did make some impact on the government and on other Americans whose critical faculties were not totally blunted by an excess of patriotism. One of the prominent national figures who demonstrated at the Pentagon, Noam Chomsky, later commented on the various anti-war activities: 'Resistance cannot now significantly deplete the manpower pool that makes possible the use of American power for global repression, nor can it, at the moment, significantly impede the research, production and supply on which this exercise of power rests. But it can contribute significantly towards raising the domestic costs of this attempt and eliminating the apathy and passivity that may permit it to succeed.'[23]

While the main opponents of the war were the young, there was much criticism also from some of the intellectuals. Such critics were not a homogeneous group. There were two broad categories of protest which have been described as 'responsible' and 'hysterical'. The 'responsible' protests came from those who did not make sweeping denunciations of the American system. They opposed the war on the purely pragmatic grounds that the cost of winning it was proving unacceptable. Arthur Schlesinger, the historian, typified that attitude. In his book *The Bitter Heritage* he questioned the conduct of the war and showed concern about its consequences in the United States, fearing, for example, that some of the war's more extreme critics might, as a result of the backlash against them, be 'preparing the way for a new McCarthyism'.[24] Schlesinger was doubtful about the judgment of a right-wing journalist that the war might, after all, be winnable. In his next sentence, however, he commented: 'We all pray that Mr. Alsop will be right.'[25] Clearly, Schlesinger had no doubt that the US was entitled to intervene in the internal affairs of Vietnam. He recognized that intervention had led to the imposition in the South of a 'régime pervaded by nepotism, corruption and cynicism'.[26] Furthermore, he admitted that, if Americans continued to pursue military victory, they would leave 'the tragic country gutted and devastated by bombs, burned by napalm, turned into a wasteland by chemical defoliation, a land of ruin and wrack'.[27] Nevertheless, he did not favour an American withdrawal from Vietnam. Instead, he recommended a more discriminating use of military power in order to 'hold the line' in the South. He still believed that the United States was entitled to use force to achieve its objective of a South Vietnamese bastion against 'international communism'.

The more extreme or 'hysterical' critics of the war denied the right of Americans to be in Vietnam at all. 'The proper question,' said one, 'is not whether the United States can win at an acceptable cost, but whether it should be involved at all in the internal affairs of Indochina.'[28] Their answer was that it should not. They appreciated, however, that the Vietnamese intervention fitted into the pattern of US policy as they perceived it. That policy, like the policy of any major power, was, in their view, determined by the 'national interest'. What constituted that interest was decided by the dominant social groups. The primary aim of those élite groups was to maximize the free access of US capital to 'the markets and human and material resources of the world' and to maintain 'its freedom of operation in a global economy'.[29] Those were the realities behind spurious claims that the Americans were acting to preserve freedom and democracy in South Vietnam. Predictably, given such a view of American motives, the radical critics were very outspoken about the intervention itself. Chomsky, for example, considered that US policy in Vietnam was no more debatable than the rape of Abyssinia by Mussolini or the Soviet intervention in Hungary in 1956. 'The war,' he said, 'is simply an obscenity, a depraved act by weak and miserable men, including all of us, who have allowed it to go on and on with endless fury and destruction – all of us who would have remained silent had stability and order been secured.'[30]

Chomsky's views were more forceful than they were representative. There were, indeed, many intellectuals who considered that even Schlesinger's much less radical strictures were unacceptable. Almost any aspersions against the generals were unwelcome to those who had made a niche in the military-industrial complex. Senator Fulbright pointed out that, since professors, no less than businessmen, liked money and influence, they were eager to accept contracts offered by the military establishment. Naturally, there were no contracts for critics and those who signed on also signed away their freedom to question the government's policies. Many in fact were prepared to be agents rather than critics of those policies: too often academic honesty was 'no less marketable than a box of detergent on the grocery shelf'.[31]

Their attitudes were shared by millions of workers, businessmen, bankers, technicians and so on who were also prospering as a result of the war economy.[32] Even in 1967 when victory still seemed elusive, public opinion remained hawkish. Harris Survey polls in February, July and August all showed that over 70 per cent of Americans supported the war. In September the figure fell to 58 per cent, but rose again to 61 per cent in December.[33] In that month delegates to the annual convention of the AFL-CIO re-affirmed overwhelmingly their support for Johnson's Vietnam policy.[34]

Johnson was aware, however, that there was widespread discontent, even if a sense of patriotism dissuaded many ordinary people from disowning their President publicly in the middle of a war. Reacting privately to the substantial number who did in fact criticize him, he complained: 'The only difference between the Kennedy assassination and mine is that I am alive and it has been more tortuous.'[35] In public, he persisted in maintaining that the enemy was 'hurting' and that victory would not be long in coming. While many Americans were prepared, like the President, to be optimistic in public, many others realized that they were being fooled. The credibility gap between the government and the governed continued to grow wider.

As the next Presidential election drew nearer there seemed little chance that Johnson could repeat the triumph he had relished four years previously. Too many things were going wrong. The President had started to build a Great Society but had been diverted from that work by the demands of the war. Such reforms as were achieved were insufficient to prevent black riots on an unprecedented scale. Millions of television sets had shown the blazing buildings of Watts and Newark. They had also shown the anti-war riots. Most important, they had taken the war itself into American homes. It may be that what the Americans did not see was more important than some of the horrors they did see. They did not see the enemy being decisively beaten, while their government claimed that victory was imminent. They saw nothing in fact to reduce the credibility gap. What they did observe was violence begetting violence, both at home and abroad. After the 1964 election Johnson might reasonably have claimed that he was at the head of an unparalleled national consensus embracing labour, the blacks, the middle class and even most of the rich. Long before 1968 that consensus was shattered. Even more seriously for

Johnson's election prospects, he had allowed the Democratic Party to disintegrate. At the beginning of 1968 the *coup de grâce* was delivered to his hopes of re-election by the Tet offensive.

For the first time, the American public saw vividly the toughness of the guerrillas not in remote jungles but in the familiar terrain of a city. 'The pictures of corpses in the garden of the American embassy cut through the haze of argument and counter-argument, giving flat contradiction to the official optimism about the slow but steady progress of the war.'[36] LBJ's credibility was blown away entirely by the Vietcong mortars in Saigon. A week after the offensive began, the journalist Art Buchwald gave the quietus to years of military dissembling in a column with the by-line 'Little Big Horn, Dakota: Gen. George Armstrong Custer said today in an exclusive interview with this correspondent that the battle of the Little Big Horn had just turned the corner and he could now see the light at the end of the tunnel. "We have the Sioux on the run", Gen. Custer told me.'[37]

By the end of March it was clear to Johnson that the prospect of his re-election was fading fast. Results of primary elections showed that the public had turned against him. As we have seen, he directed the bombing campaign away from the North and at the same time withdrew from the race for the presidency. The election campaign was eventually fought for the Democrats by Hubert Humphrey who had become prominent as a reformer but had later compromised his liberal support by a total adherence, when he was Vice-President, to Johnson's Vietnam policy. The Republican candidate was Richard Nixon, Vice-President under Eisenhower and Kennedy's rival for the presidency in 1960. His career had been built on his record as an uncompromising anti-communist and in 1968 he emphasized his opposition to radicalism with a strong commitment to 'law and order'. On Vietnam he was cagey. Feeling that Humphrey, with the albatross of LBJ's policy around his neck, was a marked man, he himself wanted to create as few vibrations as possible on that issue. His tactics seemed to be succeeding when in September the polls showed him leading Humphrey by 45 to 30 points.

Very late in the campaign, Humphrey began to disassociate himself from Johnson's stance on the war. His new posture and Nixon's continuing refusal to commit himself reduced the gap between the two men. Eventually Nixon won the election by the narrow margin of 500,000 votes in a total poll of 63 million, having by his hesitancy turned a potential landslide into a cliffhanger.[38] Both Nixon and Humphrey were party stalwarts, unlikely to make any fundamental change in America's relations with Vietnam. One candidate who might possibly have been more responsive to the public mood, Robert Kennedy, was murdered in the course of the campaign.

Nine

NIXON'S CONTINUING PURSUIT
OF VICTORY

Nixon came to power pledged to 'end the war and win the peace'. His method of winning the peace was to continue direct American involvement in the war until January 1973. During the first three years of his presidency 15,000 Americans were killed in Vietnam.[1] In the first two years the US Air Force dropped 2,539,743 million tons of bombs in Indochina – more than the total tonnage expended by America during the Second World War.[2] Within two days of taking office, Nixon ordered an incursion into Laos by a battalion of marines. (Even Johnson had refrained from a ground attack there.) The new President was, it appeared, not so much a peacemaker as a pacemaker. An American journalist noted later: 'What President Nixon means by peace is what other people mean by victory.'[3]

Johnson's experience persuaded Nixon that he must reduce the number of US ground forces in Indochina. Nevertheless he was confident that victory could be achieved; the objectives remained the same, only the means were to be modified. Thus Nixon adopted a tactic, devised first by Clifford,[4] of withdrawing American combat troops and replacing them with an expanded South Vietnamese army. 'Vietnamization' satisfied both the 'doves' who welcomed the limited US withdrawal and the 'hawks' who wished the war to continue. The American troops having failed to deliver victory, the 'Asian boys' were recruited to do their own fighting, with assistance from US technology. The new policy promised a way of defeating the enemy while keeping American casualties at an acceptable level.

A mobilization law allowed Thieu to call up all men from eighteen to thirty-eight into military service and to form self-defence units from seventeen-year-olds and men from thirty-nine to forty-three.[5] By the end of 1970 he had over a million men under his command. Moreover his troops were equipped by the

Americans with the most up-to-date automatic rifles, grenade-launchers, artillery and other weapons. They were also provided with massive air support from the US Air Force, while the South Vietnamese Air Force was also increased and a growing number of pilots trained in the USA.[6] While the effectiveness of the government forces apparently increased, the NLF had been weakened by losses sustained in 1968 and in the following year. Adams, Westmoreland's successor, carried out an Accelerated Pacification Campaign, as a result of which the Mekong Delta

19. **American marines returning home 1969.**

was seemingly cleared of the Vietcong.[7] The casualties inflicted and the devastation caused by the Ninth Division in the Delta were paralleled by the activities of the Koreans, Marines and the American Division (of My Lai fame) in large areas of central Vietnam. In the light of those events, an American officer engaged in the Vietnamization programme claimed, in October 1969, that the South Vietnamese had been given enough training and equipment to enable them to win the war.[8]

Such optimism was in fact ill-founded. The strengthening of the army merely consolidated the clique that commanded it. In 1965

George Ball, one of the few realists in Johnson's entourage, described South Vietnam as an army without a country. With Nixon's help, the army had become more effective in a military sense but remained politically isolated: it still had no country. Vietnamization simply perpetuated a situation whereby a group of Vietnamese in uniform dominated the rest of the people. It did not create a viable political alternative to the NLF.

Recognizing the political vulnerability of his ally, Nixon intensified a campaign, known as the Phoenix Programme, to destroy the infrastructure of the National Liberation Front. Instituted under American prompting and guidance in 1967, the programme was aimed at rooting out all NLF sympathizers and agents in South Vietnam. With remarkable effrontery the military dictatorship claimed that the Front's infrastructure had, by its fifth-column activities, sabotaged the country's political development. Accordingly, American and South Vietnamese security organizations co-operated to 'neutralize' the undercover Vietcong. In practice many people were liquidated who had no connection with the NLF. One intelligence officer in the US Army who was attached to the Phoenix Programme commented: 'When I arrived in the district I was given a list of 200 names of people who had to be killed. When I left after six months, we still hadn't killed anyone on the list. But we'd killed 260 other people . . .'[9] Many victims were denounced on trumped-up charges; it was an excellent opportunity for the settling of old scores. While ostensibly purging the communists, the security forces were licensed to arrest, torture and kill anyone who opposed the regime. According to the government's own figures, between 1968 and 1971, 81,039 people were convicted, some of whom 'rallied', that is, were persuaded to go over to the government side; 40,994 were killed.[10]

In March 1971 the programme was expanded at a cost to the US government of $1 billion.[11] However, despite such an enormous expenditure of money, not to mention the cost in human life, the campaign failed to destroy the NLF's basis of support. It alienated even more people than were killed and made the regime even less attractive to the ordinary citizens of South Vietnam. While the government had little success against the Front, the NLF did successfully infiltrate the regime. The CIA reported in October 1970 that within the Saigon government there were some thirty thousand people who were prepared to co-operate with the Front, and that their number might soon be fifty thousand.[12]

Despite such unpromising support, Nixon was determined to defeat the North Vietnamese, if necessary by extending the war. Thus in April 1970 he announced the US invasion of Cambodia. He claimed that his action (a 'step towards peace') was forced on him by the NVA and the NLF who were using Cambodia as a sanctuary and were a threat to its independence. It was necessary, he stated, to deny them that refuge in order to win the war in Vietnam. There was little substance in his claim. Although the NLF and their allies had crossed the border to avoid the intensive bombardment of South Vietnam, they were not attempting to seize Cambodia for their own purposes, nor were they using it as a springboard for their war in Vietnam. The border area did not indeed even offer them a very secure retreat. One eyewitness commented early in 1970 that 'there seemed no place the Vietcong could hide, let alone establish a permanent sanctuary'.[13]

In fact, what provoked American intervention in Cambodia was not so much the belligerence of the Vietcong as the neutralism of the Cambodian Head of State, Prince Sihanouk. He pointed out that for years the Americans had been pressing him to fight the NLF and that his refusal had been a major bone of contention between Phnom Penh and Washington.[14] As a result of their interference Sihanouk severed diplomatic relations in 1965. In June 1969 they were resumed in exchange for an American pledge to respect Cambodia's independence and sovereignty. Nevertheless, as a congressional committee later revealed, between March 1969 and May 1970 the Nixon administration waged a secret war against Cambodia. During that period 3,630 B-52 bombing sorties were flown over the country, their activities being concealed from Congress and the public by faking reports, burning order papers and producing false statistics.[15]

On 18 March 1970 Sihanouk was deposed while he was on a visit to Europe. Evidence presented in his book *My War with the CIA* revealed that the US Central Intelligence Agency had paved the way for his deposition. Sihanouk commented that, while the leaders of the plot, Lon Nol and Sirik Matak may have been too stupid to foresee its consequences, the United States 'consciously and deliberately, exported the war in South Vietnam to Cambodia'.[16] On

29 April South Vietnamese forces invaded Cambodia and were joined on 1 May by the Americans. The invaders provided some support for the Lon Nol regime which was under attack from pro-Sihanouk groups. They also destroyed supplies and equipment belonging to the North Vietnamese Army. Little else was achieved before increasing pressure from within the United States forced the withdrawal in July of the American troops.

In the United States the Cambodian invasion had caused widespread protests, the most tragic being at Kent State University where on 4 May Ohio National Guardsmen killed four student demonstrators. Even Congress, usually a toothless watchdog, was provoked into action. In December 1970 both Houses prohibited the introduction of US combat troops or military advisers into Cambodia. The bombing however was to continue until August 1973 when Congress finally forced Nixon to ground the bombers. In the intervening years they devastated much of the country. Even the soil itself was destroyed by a combination of bombs, napalm and chemicals. Such systematic destruction of all living things by saturation bombing caused great bitterness. Sihanouk even compared the American leadership with the Nazis. He asked '. . . what is the difference between burning and gassing people in ovens and doing it to a whole nation out in the open?

" HE TOOK THE WRAPS OFF OUR SECRET WEAPON!"

20.

That is just what the United States of President Nixon is doing today . . . Nixon is waging a war of extermination against the entire people of Indo-China.'[17]

Despite the meagre successes of his ground forces in Cambodia, and in defiance of the protests they had provoked, Nixon authorized an incursion into Laos in February 1971 by 22,000 South Vietnamese troops. Their campaign lasted a mere forty-five days and resulted in heavy casualties for the invaders. A further brief foray in May was equally unsuccessful. Such operations were justified on the grounds that Laos was being protected against invasion from North Vietnam. We might note here that American propaganda paradoxically tended to credit the North Vietnamese with the status of supermen who not only threatened South Vietnam but were also taking over Cambodia and Laos while simultaneously defending themselves against the enormous military might of the United States.[18] It is hardly surprising that convincing evidence of such ubiquitous aggression by North Vietnam was hard to find.

Hanoi did indeed provide support for the Pathet Lao, the indigenous Laotian left-wing forces; the North Vietnamese were determined to do what they could to prevent Laos from becoming a secure American base.[19] They were aware that ever since the creation of the state of Laos the US had been attempting to make it an anti-communist stronghold. From 1946 to 1963 Laos received more US aid per capita than any other country in Southeast Asia.[20] When dollars failed to ensure that Laos was a haven of US influence the American leadership resorted to force. US planes were used to attack the Pathet Lao in 1964[21] and three years later Johnson authorized the bombing of the country by B-52s. To keep their activities hidden every raid over Laos was paralleled by another over South Vietnam. As one commentator remarked, it was 'a form of information control that presumably caused, among other things, some loss of life'.[22] Nixon continued with such clandestine raids, the existence of which was at last officially admitted in 1973 at a hearing of the Senate Armed Services Committee.[23]

In Laos, as in Cambodia, the bombing intensified under Nixon – from some 4,500 sorties a month (before the November 1968 limitation of the campaign against North Vietnam) to between 12,500 and 15,000 sorties a month early in 1970.[24] In April 1970 one correspondent reported that the majority of villages and towns in Northwest Laos had been destroyed. Refugees from the Plain of Jars asserted that they had been bombed almost daily during the previous year and that they had spent most of the previous two years living in caves and holes.[25] Nixon stated in March 1970 that he was concerned about protecting American and South Vietnamese forces who were threatened by the infiltration of North Vietnamese troops and supplies along the Ho Chi Minh trail. It is worth noting that the Laotian section of that trail lay 200 miles south-east of the Plain of Jars. The scale of the bombing, moreover suggests that the US objective was not so much to protect the lives of their troops by blocking the movement of supplies but to destroy as much as possible of Laos and to force the resettlement of the population in order to weaken the revolutionary forces in the country. Although that policy killed many civilians and devastated the land, paradoxically it raised the morale of the guerrillas, making them more determined to oust a government that co-operated with the Americans.[26]

A significant feature of the American activities in Laos, Cambodia and also in Vietnam was the extent to which they were concealed from the public. The concealment practised by the administrations of Truman, Eisenhowever, Kennedy and, in particular, of President Johnson, was exposed dramatically in June 1971 with the publication by the *New York Times* of the 'Pentagon Papers'. Comprising 3,000 pages of narrative history and 4,000 pages of documents, they were a top-secret history of American involvement in Indochina from the Second World War to May 1968. This historical survey was commissioned by Secretary of Defense McNamara in 1967 when he was increasingly concerned about the war and was anxious to discover how the United States had become embroiled. Daniel Ellsberg, one of its authors, having become highly critical of a policy which previously he had supported, illegally delivered copies of most of the material to the *New York Times*. Despite attempts by the Nixon administration to prevent them, *The Times* and the *Washington Post* published the information, their action being later upheld by the Supreme Court. Their revelations about, for example, the handling of the Tonkin Gulf affair, the decision to begin Rolling Thunder, the surreptitious build-up of ground forces from 1965 and so on, have been incorporated into the present account. At the time of their publication they confirmed the suspicions and doubts of the war's critics. In the opinion of the most outspoken opponents of official policy, they 'provided documentary evidence of a conspiracy to use force in international affairs in violation of law'.[27] Even those who were not quite so hostile to the whole tenor of US policy were appalled by the deception practised upon them.[28]

Neil Sheehan, the reporter who was principally responsible for the *New York Times'* presentation of the Pentagon documents, was left with one overriding impression – that the government of the USA was not what he had thought it was. Within the government he discerned a centralized state. For the men who formed that inner government, the enemy was not merely the communists but also their own press, judiciary and Congress. They operated in secret not so much to keep hostile foreign powers in the dark as to escape judgment on their competence by their own population. Each administration avoided exposing the weaknesses of its predecessor: essentially the same people were, after all, running the successive governments. In Sheehan's opinion, such a code of secrecy encouraged underhand actions, supposedly to safeguard 'national security'. While the ordinary citizens could take pride in their democratic institutions, those at the very centre of power would do their dirty work for them. Thus the President might regale the public with disquisitions on peace, freedom and democracy while, with his closest advisers, he spoke the language of realpolitik.[29]

Many Americans were indeed unwilling to recognize some of the dreadful things that were being done, in the name of security, by their leaders. They did not wish to be shown, for example, that 'search and destroy' missions could lead to massacres such as occurred in the village of My Lai.[30] There, on 16 March 1968, American troops deliberately and indiscriminately slaughtered more than five hundred people – men, women and children. The story of the massacre was not made public until November 1969; attempts to reveal the facts previously had been thwarted.[31] When the story was eventually published many Americans refused to believe it. A poll taken in St. Louis showed that only 12 per cent of those who had heard the facts accepted them as true.[32] One reaction to the grisly story was that 'this sort of thing should have been kept classified'.[33]

Many other massacres were kept classified or were given little publicity; My Lai was by no means unique.[34] We have already seen that the American method of waging war in Indochina resulted in the wholesale killing of civilians from the air. It would be surprising to find the ground troops, who were generally at much greater risk, showing more restraint than the bomber pilots. In fact they were encouraged to regard all Vietnamese as inferiors – 'slopes', 'slant-eyes', 'gooks' and 'dinks'. (Significantly, in General Westmoreland's headquarters there were separate toilet facilities for Americans and Vietnamese.[35]) Most US soldiers followed the 'mere gook rule', according to which 'anything that moves and has a yellow skin is an enemy, unless there is incontrovertible evidence to the contrary'.[36] Conditioning them to regard the Vietnamese as sub-humans made it easier for them to kill and commit atrocities.[37] Racist attitudes, we might note, were not exclusive to the ordinary GI. Townsend Hoopes, former Under-Secretary of the Air Force and 'one of the most humane and enlightened voices to be heard within the mainstream of American opinion', commented that '. . . happiness, wealth and power are expectations that constitute a dimension far beyond the experience, and probably beyond the emotional comprehension of the Asian poor'.[38] His assumption that peasants in Asia are incapable of happiness is on a par with a belief common in the West that life is cheap to Asians, that they are cruel and barbaric to their own people and that they do not share civilized Western values. Similar assumptions were made about American Indians: the mass slaughter of the Indians found a parallel in the ruthlessness shown to the Vietnamese.[39] One American commentator was prompted to ask: 'would we have pursued quite such policies – and quite such military tactics – if the Vietnamese were white?'[40]

The tactic of indiscriminate killing was not only a crime but also a blunder. Many Vietnamese, and Laotians and Cambodians, were convinced that the US was launched on a course of genocide. Believing that, they were constrained to fight back, whatever the odds. The simple desire for self-preservation (they did, *pace* Hoopes, care for life) helped to explain the remarkable resilience of the NLF and the North Vietnamese. So resilient were they that by the spring of 1972 they were ready to begin a new major offensive in South Vietnam, where conditions were giving cause for alarm to those with eyes to see. One American correspondent observed: 'It could be as long as two or three years before the

Reds take over. But it could be this summer or as early as Tet.'[41]

The economic situation in South Vietnam had suffered as a result of the withdrawal of American forces and the consequent reduction of the flow of US dollars. Inflation was a major problem and it was expected that by the summer of 1972 the government would start simply printing money to pay its bills.[42] The closure of American bases also added to the considerable number of the unemployed. Furthermore, of the population of 17 million people some 5 million were refugees, many of whom lived in and around the cities and towns. As a result of the widespread destruction of the countryside, South Vietnam was more urbanized than Switzerland.[43] Ex-peasants huddled together in shanty towns, dependent on hand-outs for their survival. Economic grievances were compounded by political repression. Commenting on the condition of his country a Vietnamese doctor pointed out that 'the counter appeal to communism must be material or moral. But on the one hand are rising prices, unemployment. On the other, corruption, no real democracy, above all, no real patriotism.'[44]

The despair of the South Vietnamese was matched by the low morale of the remaining American troops, their discipline undermined by 'radical politics, racial tension and sheer indifference'.[45] Officers and NCOs were chary of exercising their authority for fear of being 'fragged', that is, attacked by their own men with fragmentation grenades. Drug taking among the troops was endemic. Smoking 'pot' was commonplace and in May 1971 the Army Secretary stated that there was between 10 and 15 per cent hard drug addiction in the Vietnam command.[46]

The brunt of the 1972 spring offensive was borne not by the demoralized Americans but by the equally despondent army of South Vietnam. What little enthusiasm they had for the war was shattered by General Giap's 130 mm guns. After the fall of Quang Tri the remaining soldiers of the 3rd. Division and the Rangers went wild with panic and fled, leaving their wounded to die by the roadside.[47] After a disastrous opening phase the South Vietnamese leadership did recover its nerve. Furthermore, the US intensified its bombing campaign: in April Nixon rseumed the bombing of North Vietnam. Giap's offensive did not, as initially seemed likely, sweep all before it. Nevertheless the NLF and the North Vietnamese Army made considerable gains. By October the army of South Vietnam was short of strategic fighting units;

those remaining were unable to recapture the 'liberated' areas. In one month the Vietcong, having drawn away the main units of Thieu's army, had assumed control of the Delta. Divisions of the North Vietnamese Army were massing on the border with Cambodia. The senior American adviser in the Delta considered that the situation was 'back where it was in 1965'.[48]

The enemy's successes were of particular concern to Nixon since the presidential election was due in November. The Watergate affair has revealed how determined he was to be re-elected. In February 1972, for example, his associates forged letters to discredit Senator Muskie, one of the contenders for the nomination of the Democratic Party. Senator McGovern, Nixon's eventual challenger, had long been opposed to the Vietnam War which he promised to end quickly if elected. Nixon sought to undermine McGovern not only by corrupting the electoral process but also by attempting to resolve the issue of the war before the election. His response to the enemy's spring offensive was to bomb Hanoi into submission. Evidently he still believed that victory could be achieved if sufficient force were applied against North Vietnam. His new offensive was even more concentrated than the bombing carried out under Johnson. There were virtually no restrictions on targets: Hanoi and Haiphong were attacked immediately. Nixon even agreed to the mining of North Vietnamese ports, a move Johnson had eschewed because of its possible international repercussions. Littauer, an authority on the air-war, pointed out in May 1972 that the US was dropping 3,000 tons per day on Indochina, at a daily cost of $20 million.[49] The raids on the North quickly negated the enormous effort at reconstruction made there since the end of the 1968 offensive – new port facilities, roads and bridges were some of the targets destroyed. According to the Swedish Chargé d'Affaires in Hanoi, the bombers 'had hit everything worth hitting'.[50] A French eyewitness reported that Nam Dinh, the third largest city in North Vietnam, was four-fifths destroyed. Shops, schools, flats and most of a 300-bed hospital were flattened by raid after raid. In the end it appeared that the US pilots were intent on simply pulverizing the ruins.[51]

Remarkably, morale remained high and the war effort continued. In Nam Dinh, for example, essential services were organized underground or dispersed in the neighbouring countryside. After the destruction of a large textile mill, production continued in ten thatched buildings outside the city.[52] The toughness and ingenuity of the North Vietnamese greatly reduced the military effectiveness of the bombing, although a great price had to be paid in lost lives, injury and material destruction. The bombing did not prevent a good harvest, a point of crucial importance in a land where 90 per cent of the population lived in the countryside.

Given the failure of the air offensive to enforce the capitulation of North Vietnam and bearing in mind the desperate situation in the South, Nixon was constrained to try another tactic before the Americans went to the polls. For years peace talks had dragged on fruitlessly in Paris. In October 1972 the President allowed Kissinger his principal adviser on foreign policy, to negotiate a draft agreement with the North Vietnamese on ending hostilities. Its terms were published shortly before the presidential election and bombing above the 20th parallel was restricted. The public in the United States and indeed throughout the world were led to believe that peace was imminent. McGovern's lack-lustre campaign had already indicated that Nixon would have an easy victory. Kissinger's manoeuvrings in Paris ensured him a landslide, in which he gained a majority in 49 of the 50 states, on 7 November.

The American government had delayed signing the draft agreement before Nixon's re-election. After the victory was won Kissinger was given a new brief which was, in effect, to repudiate the agreement they had previously accepted. Under Point 1 of the draft, the United States had respected the unity of Vietnam as recognized by the 1954 Geneva Agreement. In December, however, Kissinger insisted that Hanoi accept at least implicitly the division of Vietnam and thus the sovereignty of Thieu's government in the South.[53] It would appear that the October negotiations had been occasioned not so much by a genuine concern to end the fighting as by electoral expediency on the part of the Nixon administration. When the North Vietnamese refused to accept the new terms negotiations broke down and Nixon began a further air attack against the North which outdid in intensity even the formidable bombardment of the summer.

During the first week of the new campaign 18,000 tons of bombs were dropped on North Vietnam.[54] Two French journalists in Hanoi, a city of 1 million people, were told that the bombing was killing 200 and wounding 200 of its inhabitants every day. They observed the bombed ruins of Bach Mai hospital, noting wryly the Pentagon claim that no civilian objective in Hanoi had been destroyed by bombs. They stated that the Kham Tien quarter, with 28,000 inhabitants, had been 'ground to nothing by night carpet-bombing'. The B-52s had devastated an area one and half miles long and several hundred yards wide, where most of the houses had been atomized.[55] As information about the damage was published there was widespread criticism in the United States and in many other countries. In Britain, Professor Denis Brogan, one of the foremost authorities on and a life-long friend of the USA, expressed his outrage at a policy which, sustained for a number of years and then renewed with unprecedented violence, appeared 'to be equal to any of the war crimes for which high-ranking German or Japanese officers were executed after the Second World War'.[56]

Nixon's latest turn of the screw was short-lived. Early in January 1973 negotiations were resumed and at the end of the month a ceasefire was agreed by both sides. It has been commonly assumed that, since the renewal of negotiations followed so soon after the Christmas bombing, Nixon's tactics, however repugnant, were at least effective. Several considerations cast doubt on that assumption. First, the morale in the North remained high even at the height of the bombing. An American clergyman wrote from Hanoi at the end of the first week of the latest offensive: 'So life goes on here. The streets still are full of bicycles and the children still smile as we four Americans pass by. But many people are being evacuated. They say everything of any strategic worth has long since gone. There are only the people, and I see no signs of weakening. They say they have fought for independence for 1,000 years and they won't stop now.'[57] One of the reasons for their impressive belligerence was the sudden vulnerability of the B-52s. During the first week of the December raids the North Vietnamese shot down ten, each costing £3,400,000.[58] Their sharpshooting gravely embarrassed the American President. Since coming to power he had used every practicable resource available in his quest for victory. Cambodia and Laos had been invaded, Haiphong harbour had been mined, unrestricted air-war had been waged against all Indochina. For obvious reasons the use of nuclear weapons and a massive re-deployment of US ground troops were ruled out. With characteristic tenacity Nixon had done his utmost to win a war which in 1968 Johnson and many other Americans

CHINA

Red R.

NORTH

• Dien Bien Phu

Hanoi • • Haiphong

Gulf of Tongking

L

VIETNAM

U.S. 7th fleet bombs and shells North Vietnam

Vientiane •

R. Mekong

A

17th Parallel

Hue

THAILAND

O

★ Da Nang

B52 airstrikes from Guam

★ Utapao

B52 airstrikes from Thailand

S

SOUTH

CAMBODIA

VIETNAM

★ NhaTrang

Phnom Penh •

Bien Hoa

Saigon

Ho Chi Minh trail

★ Major U.S. basis

Areas largely controlled by Vietcong, 1973

| 0 | km | 300 |
| 0 | miles | 200 |

★ Cai Ngai

had recognized as unwinnable. By 1973 even he was convinced that direct military intervention by the United States should be abandoned.

Obviously the North Vietnamese were relieved when the bombing ended but they had not resumed negotiations simply to obtain that relief. The fact was that the Nixon–Kissinger tactic of the carpet-bombing of urban centres failed. In January they were obliged to accept (although, as we shall see, with the greatest cynicism) an agreement which was virtually identical to the proposals Hanoi had put forward the previous October.[59]

Ten

THE END OF THE WAR

The crucial statement in the Paris Agreement, signed on 27 January 1973, was as follows: 'The United States and all other countries respect the independence, sovereignty, unity and territorial integrity of Vietnam as recognized by the 1954 Geneva Agreements on Vietnam.' Unity would be achieved by a reunification of the North and the South 'carried out step by step through peaceful negotiations'. In the South there was to be established a National Council of National Reconciliation and Concord, including representatives of the Saigon Government, the Provisional Revolutionary Government, which since 1969 had been the political organ of the guerrilla forces opposed to Saigon, and also of the Third Force – the non-communist critics of the Thieu regime. The council was to implement the agreement by guaranteeing freedom of the press, of assembly, of organization and of political activity. It was also to organize, within ninety days, free and democratic elections. Within sixty days all US and allied troops were to be withdrawn from South Vietnam; North Vietnamese troops fighting alongside the PRG were, however, allowed to stay.[1]

It was generally appreciated that, if the terms of the agreement were carried out, Thieu's regime would come to a sudden end. Aware of this probability, he had issued, before the ceasefire went into effect, a 'flurry of decrees' that negated its provisions. 'Neutralist and pro-communist elements', that is any opponents of the government, were to be imprisoned. Even more newspapers were closed, more people jailed for trying to hold political meetings and all opposition parties declared to be illegal. In December 1972 an American observer remarked that not since the time of Ngo Dinh Diem had South Vietnam seen 'such wholesale arrests, crackdown on the press and other repressive measures'.[2]

While Thieu was doing his utmost to conceal the facts from

the people of South Vietnam, his opponents distributed millions of copies of the ceasefire agreement. The PRG and its allies were justifiably confident that 'nothing could prevent their ultimate victory if, after the Paris ceasefire, the struggle for Vietnam became primarily a political contest'.[3]

President Nixon, in order to avoid that outcome, had assured Thieu that he would have the full support of the United States in blocking any form of political settlement and in continuing the military offensive against the PRG. Even before the agreement was concluded Nixon had strengthened his ally's hand. Since October 1972 extra supplies had been shipped to the forces of South Vietnam. Thus, at the time of the ceasefire, Thieu's air force consisted of some 550 fixed-wing aircraft and 1,100 helicopters. The delivery of new weapons to his army allowed it to contemplate the outbreak of peace behind the barrels of 2,500 artillery pieces and 800 tanks. In addition, his generals had at their disposal supplies sufficient to equip some two million soldiers.[4]

Maynard Parker, an American commentator who supported US policy in Vietnam, subsequently admitted that the re-equipping of South Vietnam's armed services was a prelude to sabotaging the ceasefire: 'Almost from the moment the agreement was signed, President Thieu, realizing that the balance of power was in his favour, took the offensive in an attempt to eradicate the Communist inkspots and confine the Communists to their sanctuaries.'[5] Anxious not to give Thieu any excuse for claiming that his moves were merely defensive, or to allow him any justification for officially terminating the ceasefire, the People's Liberation Army permitted the South Vietnamese to occupy numerous areas in zones accepted as being under the control of the PRG. Only some guerrillas and local troops resisted these clear breaches of the agreement.

However, while Thieu made some territorial gains during the summer of 1973, he also suffered a major reverse at the hands of the US Congress. Nixon's bombing campaign of December 1972 aroused, as we have seen, intense public opposition and provoked a reaction from the representatives of the American people. On 31 July 1973 Congress voted to end all bombing in Indochina by US forces and to prohibit any future military operations there without Congressional approval. That decision made it more difficult for Nixon to give the full backing that he had promised

the Saigon regime. Since he had no other option, Thieu nevertheless was obliged to persist with his strong-arm tactics in the hope
that a major Communist counter-attack would persuade Congressmen to change their minds. In August he moved two
regiments of the 22nd Infantry Division and three battalions of
Rangers into northern Binh Dinh province. There they seized
20 square miles of rice land from the PRG in an offensive of
such scale that some American officials expected a comparable
response from the Communists. In October the editor of a Third
Force journal remarked that 'the Thieu regime has done everything possible to destroy the peace and provoke a full scale resump-
tion of the war'.[6]

Eventually the Communists did hit back. On 11 October an
order of the day authorized the People's Liberation Army to resist
the land-grabbing operations of the enemy and to retaliate against
their rear bases. In November 1973 a major offensive was launched
in Quang Duc, including a rocket attack on Bien Hoa air base.
Thieu's supporters in the Pentagon and the State Department
cited these actions as harbingers of extensive Communist counter-
attacks within the next two or three months. There was, however,
no evidence for their view. On the contrary, US intelligence
officials had learned that no general Communist offensive was
being planned for 1974: the Communists were still intent on
manoeuvring the Saigon government into complying with the
Paris Agreement.

For his part, Thieu was openly contemptuous of that agreement.
At the end of December he said that there would be no general
election, as had been stipulated, nor any negotiated settlement.
On 4 January 1974 he declared bluntly: 'As far as the armed
services are concerned, I can tell you the war has restarted.'[7]
Within the next few months both sides did in fact increase their
military activities and in May the political and military talks
between them completely broke down.

During July and August the US Congress agreed an allocation
of $770 million for military aid, instead of the $1.4 billion requested
by Nixon, expressing the hope that such a reduction would put
pressure on Thieu to negotiate a solution. While he refused to
oblige the Congressmen, they were equally unwilling to counten-
ance any renewal of American military involvement in the war.
Thieu's hopes suffered an additional set-back in August when

Nixon, in the aftermath of the Watergate scandal,* had to resign in disgrace. The leaders of the Lao Dong Party commented that his resignation had adversely affected the Saigon administration in all respects and had driven 'henchman Nguyen Van Thieu into a state of confusion'.[8] Early in the new year they declared that Thieu would continue to sustain major defeats until a government willing to implement the Paris Agreement replaced him.

How much the balance of power was tilting against his regime was evident in December 1974 when a twelve-day offensive gave the PRG control of Phuoc Long province, with the exception of its capital Phuoc Binh, which was itself captured on 7 January. From 18 December to 8 January 1975 the North Vietnamese Politbureau met to decide the strategy of a major campaign against the Saigon government. The outcome was a two-year plan which General Van Tien Dung, then Chief of Staff of the Vietnam People's Army, described as follows: '... in 1975 we would strike unexpectedly with large, widespread offensives, and create conditions to carry out a general offensive and uprising in 1976. In 1976 we would launch the general offensive and uprising to liberate the South completely.' He added that 'the Political Bureau had foreseen another tendency and included in the 1975 plan another essential course of action: if the opportune moment presents itself at the beginning or the end of 1975, we will immediately liberate the South in 1975.'[9]

The first success of the campaign was the capture, between 10–11 March, of Ban Me Thuot, headquarters of the 23rd Division of the army of South Vietnam and unofficial capital of the Central Highlands. In the view of Van Tien Dung, its quick collapse 'threw the enemy into panic and confusion. . . . From tactical and campaign errors, the enemy went on to make strategic errors under our painful blows; the panicked Saigon administration issued orders to flee from the Tay Nguyen [Central Highlands] and bring their troops to the plains in order to preserve their forces and hold onto their territory. . . . After this strategic mistake. defeat in the war was certain; it was only a matter of time.'[10]

By 19 March virtually the whole of the Central Highlands had been liberated: in less than three weeks the Saigon government had lost control of an area of 18,532 square miles with a population

---

* On that major political scandal see D. Snowman, *America since 1920* (Heinemann Educational Books, 1978) pp. 191 ff.

of 800,000. The swift advance of the PRG forces was made possible by the support they received from the local inhabitants and also by the total demoralization of the enemy, who often fled without offering any significant resistance. At Hué on 25 March, the PLA having penetrated the city, the Saigon troops precipitately withdrew to the coast, where within the next few days many surrendered. At Danang the discipline of the South Vietnamese forces disintegrated even before they made contact with the enemy. 'Thousands of soldiers, many of them in stolen civilian clothes, not only looted all over town, sacking hospitals and stealing drugs: they also shot civilians, including children. The streets of Danang were littered with bodies.'[11] Faced by such ineffectual opposition the Communists destroyed and dispersed 100,000 enemy troops within thirty-two hours. Thus by 29 March they had taken over the second largest city in the South, a strong combined-forces base, and in so doing had acquired about $300 million-worth of military equipment.

So spectacular was the progress made since the opening of the campaign that the Politbureau of the Lao Dong Party decided that Saigon was to be liberated before the beginning of the next rainy season. That decision was made on 25 March. Danang fell, as we have seen, on 29 March and thereafter a rapid advance was made along the coast. Quy Nhon was captured on 1 April, as was Tuy Hoa. On 3 April the huge naval base at Cam Ranh was liberated. President Ford, on the same day, remarked that he 'did not anticipate the fall of South Vietnam'.[12]

Despite that high-placed, and misplaced, optimism in Washington, the Saigon leaders knew that on the battlefield some forceful action was needed to raise the morale of their troops. (Thieu's own morale was by no means enhanced when on 8 April his Independence Palace in Saigon was bombed by Nguyen Thanh Trung, a Communist who had infiltrated the South Vietnamese Air Force and had then rejoined his comrades taking his aircraft with him.) In order to stop the rot and to block the road to Saigon, the bulk of the South's forces were concentrated at Xuan Loc. General Le Minh Dao, one of the best of its senior officers, was given command of the defence zone and pledged to defend it to the death. For once the South Vietnamese army did stand and fight. The battle for Xuan Loc lasted from 9 April until 20 April when Thieu's forces, in imminent danger of being surrounded then annihilated, were forced to abandon the city and fled in confusion towards Ba Ria.

Once in control of Xuan Loc, the Communist leaders put the finishing touches to their preparations for the attack on Saigon itself. According to Van Tien Dung, their broad aims were: to move fast and be certain of victory when they attacked; to 'open a path to life' for the great mass of the enemy troops and not to destroy their lives 'once they had laid down their weapons, surrendered and escaped the grip of their leaders, these hirelings of the Americans'; and to liberate the millions of their compatriots in the city without making them endure any great loss of life or property. When Dung was asked subsequently what had been his most difficult decision during the Great Spring Offensive he replied: 'How to take Saigon with minimum bloodshed.'[13]

The disarray among the Saigon leadership made his task easier. On 21 April Thieu had resigned, complaining vehemently about his 'betrayal' by the Americans. He was replaced for a few days by Vice President Tran Van Huong who, against all reason, insisted on continuing the war. On 26 April at 5 p.m. the final offensive against Saigon, called the 'Ho Chi Minh Campaign', was launched. On the same day, Thieu fled with his family and belongings, including 16 tons of gold and silver, to Taiwan. After manoeuvring among various political groups in Saigon, on 27 April the two houses of the National Assembly met to accept the resignation of Tran Van Huong and to invest Duong Van Minh as president.

The new president and his ministers governed nobody. The Communist forces on 27 April had cut Highway 15, linking Saigon to Vung Tau, which fell on 28 April: they thus controlled communications between Saigon and the sea. Also on 28 April they occupied Phu Lam, which lay $5\frac{1}{2}$ miles from the capital, and Hanh Thong Tay, in its suburbs. On 29 April their aircraft bombed the big air base of Tan Son Nhat, which was already under rocket and shelling attack. During the night of 29–30 April they stormed the paratroop base in the centre of Saigon and occupied Tan Son Nhat, the headquarters of the South Vietnamese Army and other important posts.

This rapidity of movement by the PRG forces left the enemy bewildered. In the last remaining hours of the Saigon regime the Americans were reduced to evacuating by helicopter their embassy staff and other personnel from various rooftops in the city. Their ambassador, Graham Martin, who had consistently refused to take seriously CIA reports of the collapse of the morale of the South Vietnamese Army, was forced to leave Saigon at 3.30 in the morning of 30 April. Eight hours later a column of tanks arrived at the Independence Palace, the presidential residence, where the raising of the PRG flag signalled the transfer of power within the capital. After the collapse of Saigon the remaining South Vietnamese troops quickly surrendered and by 1 May the PRG was master of the Mekong Delta. On 7 March 1975 it had controlled only a single province: by 1 May it had taken over all forty-four provinces of South Vietnam. Without doubt the Great Spring Offensive was one of the most remarkable campaigns in military history. It was also the culmination of an impressive record of resistance by revolutionary nationalists in Vietnam to the intervention of two major colonial powers and to the puppet regimes they created. The remarkable fact was that Vietnam, a small, impoverished country, had thwarted the world's most economically and militarily powerful nation. There were a number of reasons for this unlikely victory.

We have already noted that there was substantial opposition to the Vietnam War within the United States itself. While it is true that many people turned against the war only because too many young Americans were being killed, there were also those who protested against the abuse of power by their own country. On the morrow of the final collapse of the Saigon regime one such opponent commented:

> ... we should not only remember the vast destruction that our massive military machine caused. We can also be proud of helping to stop the destruction. We have more heroes from the war in Vietnam than any other war in our history ... There were thousands of men who refused to co-operate with the Selective Service system – and millions of women, men and children who marched the streets of Washington, New York, Peoria, Boston and San Francisco, shouting 'Stop this war'.[14]

Such antipathy within the United States to the policies of success-ive governments encouraged the Vietnamese to persist in their unequal struggle.

They were heartened also by substantial economic and military aid from the Soviet Union and China; without that support the Vietnamese war effort could scarcely have been sustained. While recognizing that fact we should, however, bear in mind that much more help was given by the Americans to the Saigon regime. The Indochina Resources Centre in Washington reported in January 1975 that, while aid from China and the USSR to North Vietnam since January 1973 amounted to less than $1.5 billion, during the same period the United States had expended over $7 billion in maintaining the South. Buttinger has calculated that during the full course of the war South Vietnam received from the United States more than five times the amount sent to the Vietnamese Communists by Moscow and Peking.[15]

As we have seen, even those vast sums could not buy victory. The Great Spring Offensive showed beyond question that morale was more important than material and that the morale of the revolutionaries was incomparably higher than that of the Saigon troops. In examining why that was the case we come to the principal reason for the success of those opposed to the United States and its puppets. The fact was that the Americans were in conflict not with a small, unrepresentative clique but with the tremendous force of Vietnamese nationalism, harnessed at this stage in its history by leaders who espoused both nationalism and socialism; who felt themselves following not only in the footsteps of Karl Marx but also in the procession of Vietnamese patriots who had lived long before the October Revolution. Some time after the end of the Spring Offensive Van Tien Dung was asked to what extent the strategies and tactics employed in that campaign had been influenced by those of other great battles in the history of Vietnam. 'But this was the great culmination', he replied, 'of the experiences of all the battles fought by our ancestors.'[16] This was not just rhetoric but an expression of the fact that Dung was not only a Communist but a Vietnamese Communist, and that his inheritance from his ancestors was as significant as the legacy of Lenin. To the same questioner, Dung, in explaining the different tasks of the army, pointed out that 'wherever they are – in the fields or forests or on irrigation projects – the ... officers and men never lose sight of their main role, defence of the Fatherland'.[17] Not, we might note, the advancement of world revolution.

Successive American leaders failed to appreciate how deeply

ingrained in the Vietnamese was the habit of resisting aggression. The author of *Our Military Traditions*, a pamphlet recently published in Hanoi, begins with the statement that in the tenth and eleventh centuries the Chinese feudal Sung dynasty twice tried to invade Vietnam; he then goes on to describe some notable Vietnamese victories, beginning in 1077 and ending in 1789.[18] His pamphlet is a reminder that when the American Constitution was brand-new the Vietnamese had already had 800 years' experience of fighting for their independence. In more recent times they have been struggling since 1859 to regain their freedom from colonial exploitation. Always they have adopted an attitude of mind which makes defeat unthinkable. An American missionary who, towards the end of the war in 1975, came to know some of his country's enemies, remarked on their 'unshakeable conviction that their cause was "just" and that, regardless of the obstacles, it would eventually prevail. The cause would *have* to prevail because it was a "righteous cause".' Among the revolutionaries he discovered 'an undauntable belief in the mission that I had rarely encountered in five years of meeting ARVN soldiers. Even more seldom, as I remembered, among American soldiers in Vietnam.'[19]

The consequences of the Vietnamese victory were as far-reaching as its causes were deep-rooted. According to one observer, it 'broke the hegemony of the United States over the post-war world'.[20] While that comment overstates the case, the collapse of the Saigon regime did have repercussions well beyond the frontiers of Vietnam. Burchett, a veteran supporter of the Vietnamese revolution, has asserted: 'Wherever in the world people struggle for national liberation and independence, it is Vietnam which is taken as an exemplary model of "how to do it".'[21] Even less sympathetic commentators have recognized the impact of the victory on the rest of Southeast Asia. Lewy, for example, has pointed out that it was 'soon followed by a communist takeover in Laos' and that the Thais forthwith asked US troops to leave their country; furthermore, that the government of the Philippines requested a review of the status of American bases on its territory and that even in the rigidly anti-communist Indonesia, the foreign minister, Adam Malik, anticipated that he would be obliged to co-operate with the communist regimes that had established themselves in Indochina. Malik also observed that the Saigon government had expected too much of the Americans but that others would not make that mistake.[22]

Apprehension that potential allies might doubt the reliability of US governments was one of the reactions in the United States itself to the end of the Vietnam War. Furthermore, while there was considerable relief, since it had been the longest and most unpopular war in American history, there was also concern about the seeming impotence of American power against a small and impoverished adversary. Inevitably, the military establishment complained that they had been stabbed in the back by the politicians who had prevented them from using all the means at their disposal. They were apparently incapable of appreciating what comprehensive devastation had in fact been visited on Vietnam or of understanding that the enemy would have continued to resist no matter what degree of force had been deployed against them.

Some notable politicians shared their illusions. Buttinger has noted that, in an address to Veterans of Foreign Wars, Ronald Reagan, then aspiring to the presidency, accused the Federal Government of having 'walked away' from the Vietnam War. 'Either he actually believes,' said Buttinger, 'that Johnson, Nixon and Ford would not let our armed forces in Vietnam win the war, a belief which should finish him as their chief spokesman even in the eyes of his conservative followers; or he really knows better, revealing with his strange statement a truly outrageous degree of political irresponsibility.'[23]

As a critic of the war, Buttinger himself wanted the United States to 'correct past errors and repair past wrongs'. He shared the hope of some of his fellow Americans that, in a shorter time than it took to come to terms with Communist China, the United States would establish a new relationship with the Communist Vietnamese and help to rebuild the country they had devastated. However, he feared that no real progress would be made unless American leaders recognized that their Vietnam policy had been wrong from the very beginning.[24]

Even in the early post-war days his hopes were proving illusory and his fears being realized. On the very day the PRG flag was being hoisted over Saigon, the *Washington Post* declared that, although 'much of the actual conduct of Vietnam policy over the years was wrong and misguided – even tragic – it cannot be denied that some part of the purpose of that policy was right and defensible. Specifically, it was right to hope that the people of South Vietnam would be able to decide on their own form of government and social order.'[25] Even one of the most influential organs of 'liberal' opinion in the United States had manifestly learned little from the experience of Vietnam. Implicit in its statement is an assumption that it was natural and 'moral' for Americans to intervene in Vietnam. Characteristically, the motive for intervention was said to be a concern for the right of people to choose their own form of government. Also typical was the misinterpretation of the circumstances. The *Post* ignored the fact that South Vietnam was not a nation with genuine roots in Vietnamese history but a client state, created by the United States itself in the wake of the Geneva Accords of 1954. It also neglected to remind its readers that, thanks to American support, Ngo Dinh Diem was able to prevent the holding of elections in 1956, at which the people should have elected a government for the whole country.

The stance taken by the *Post* in criticizing the conduct of the war while arguing that, in some respects, US leaders were acting with laudable intentions, has been adopted also by others. Thus Lewy states that the United States 'fought a limited [sic] war whose rationale was never convincingly explained and which, in any event, even an able leader would have had a most difficult time justifying'. Nevertheless, he believes that 'the sad fate of the people of Indochina since 1975 lends strength to the view that the American attempt to prevent a communist domination of the area was not without moral justification'.[26]

Notwithstanding the experience in Vietnam, there is a common assumption in the United States that, regardless of other considerations – including the sovereignty of nations – American leaders are justified in combating what they identify as the 'evils of communism' wherever they appear. According to certain critics of US policy, that is the reality behind the rhetoric about the 'Free World' and 'human rights'. Contending that the setback in Vietnam would not have a lasting effect, Chomsky and Herman predict that in all likelihood

traditional US government policies of international subversion and – when circumstances warrant – overt aggression will continue so as 'to ensure access to vital resources or to protect embattled investments abroad' or the opportunity for future expansion of US-based capital. The sources of these programs have undergone no significant change. And the intelligentsia can be expected to resume their traditional role, somewhat eclipsed with the trauma of the war in Indochina, in support of state violence and terror. They will construct an appropriate version of history and an interpretation of the contemporary world that will enlist popular support for these programs, or at least ensure a requisite degree of passivity and unconcern.[27]

Before considering how far this sombre forecast was borne out by events in the period 1975 to 1980, we look briefly at one important result of the intransigence of the US government in the years up to 1975. As we have seen, the non-communist Third Force, composed of well-known Buddhists, Catholics, labour leaders and even former military commanders, was, at the time of the Paris Agreement, due to be included in a National Council of National Reconciliation. The Communists in South Vietnam were, indeed, prepared to form a coalition government, including Third Force representatives, after the elections organized by the National Council. However, as a result of the obduracy of Thieu, prompted and backed by Nixon, no elections were held and the Communists were driven to seek a military solution which gave them an overwhelming victory. Thus they no longer had any reason to accept a compromise which would have given an important, even if transitional, role to the Third Force. Consequently, from May 1975, the Communists were the only political force of any significance in Vietnam. How they tackled the problems of reconstruction and reunification is the main theme of Chapter 11.

Eleven

REUNIFICATION AND THE BEGINNING OF RECONSTRUCTION

Although it failed to subdue its enemies, the US war machine did succeed in devastating much of Vietnam and in killing and maiming many of its people. John Pilger, visiting the country two and a half years after the war ended, reported that 'much of North Vietnam is a moonscape from which visible signs of life – houses, factories, schools, hospitals, pagodas, churches – have been obliterated. In some forests there are no longer birds and animals; and there are lorry drivers who will not respond to the hooting of a horn because they are deaf from the incessant sound of bombs.' According to the Vietnamese authorities, the 1972 bombings alone caused 30,000 cases of permanent deafness among children. Another by-product of the bombing discovered by Pilger was the persistent action of napalm which, he said, 'continues to smoulder under the skin's tissues through the lifetime of its victims' – that is, those victims who had not already perished. The incredible intensity of the material destruction was evident in the city of Vinh where not even the foundations of the buildings remained to be seen.[1]

In South Vietnam the US Air Force contrived an additional form of destruction to supplement the damage done by its high explosives and incendiaries: it sprayed more than 100,000 tons of toxic chemicals. Seventy per cent of the coconut orchards, 60 per cent of rubber plantations, 110,000 acres of pine forests and 150,000 acres of mangrove forests were attacked with defoliants. As a result of the spraying a quantity of food sufficient to feed millions of people was destroyed. The chemicals also claimed 2 million human victims, including 3,500 dead.[2] Although intended to destroy the forests that gave sanctuary to the enemies of the United States, they also affected the American forces themselves. In February 1980 a report in the British press pointed out: 'For many of the Americans who fought in it, the Vietnam War may not be over. More than ten years after the event, the use of chemical defoliants upon millions of acres of Vietnamese country-side is alleged to be bringing death and destruction to thousands of young Americans who thought they were survivors.'[3] In the American press during the same month it was reported that the Veterans Administration had received at least 5,000 claims for sickness and disablement caused by a defoliant called Agent Orange, containing the highly toxic substance dioxin.[4]

As a result of intensive bombing and of the carefully planned destruction of forests and arable land, the peasants of South Vietnam were driven to the cities. This deliberate policy of urbanization was intended to dry up the 'sea' within which the guerrillas operated. It succeeded not only in hindering the enemy during the war but in creating a plethora of social problems which the new regime had to tackle once the war was over. They were to be seen most conspicuously in Saigon. Reviewing what confronted him in the spring of 1975, Dr Nguyen Van Thu, the member of the Saigon Military Management Committee respons-ible for health and social affairs, observed: 'We found all sorts of epidemic diseases when we arrived, including cholera, typhoid, plague – not to mention venereal disease and drug addicts – especially those on heroin.'[5] There were some 130,000 drug addicts in the city; between 100,000 and 300,000 prostitutes (it was not easy to determine how many were practising the 'profes-sion' part time); about 300,000 thieves and pickpockets; and also some 280,000 orphans fathered by Americans, Australians, Thais, Filipinos, Koreans and Taiwan Chinese – all left unprovided for. Such, noted Dr Thu, was part of the legacy of the US–Saigon regime.

Other aspects of the new government's inheritance were unemployment and inflation. Huyn Tan Phat, Prime Minister of the PRG, claimed that there was a total of 3.5 million unemployed in South Vietnam. Over a million had been unemployed before the PRG victory: that figure was enlarged first by the withdrawal of the Americans, whose presence had created many jobs, and then by the disbanding of the South Vietnamese armed forces. In addition, the economy was plagued by galloping inflation: the currency had been devalued almost every week prior to 30 April 1975; furthermore, the bank vaults had been emptied of their gold and foreign exchange reserves. Drastic inflation had, in fact, helped to weaken the previous regime. In mid-1974 92 per cent of the South Vietnamese troops surveyed by the US Defense Attaché's Office stated that, because of inflation, their pay and allowances were inadequate to provide food, clothing and shelter for their families.[6]

The economy of South Vietnam had been wholly dependent on the outside aid which had created and maintained the vast military machine required by US policy. With the withdrawal of the annual subsidy of $700 million from the United States its mainstay disappeared. The transitional difficulties, until such time as a radically different kind of economy could be established, were bound to be enormous. Noting some of them, Nayan Chanda, the principal Vietnam correspondent of the *Far Eastern Economic Review*, wrote in May 1975:

Hanoi's main problem after the capture of the whole of the South is likely to be a desperate shortage of oil and petroleum products. The farmers in the southern half of the country are used to mechanized farming and modern transport.... Hanoi cannot hope to induce China to boost oil supplies ... and will have to look elsewhere for the sort of oil imports the South has enjoyed in the past. Foreign exchange headaches of a monumental order will then arise.[7]

Other examples of problems generated by the immensely protracted conflict that had raged in Vietnam could be multiplied almost unendingly. Clearly the challenges of reconstruction were likely to be almost as demanding as the war itself. The condition of just one province in the South illustrates how much had to be done in village after village throughout the whole of the countryside.

When peace came to Nghia Binh Province, out of a total of 741,000 acres of agricultural land, more than 123,000 were lying waste or fallow. Everywhere there were barbed-wire fences, mines and unexploded bombs: in courtyards, in gardens, in the fields, on the paths along boundaries between the ricefields, in the hills and along the roadsides. Some 600,000 of the inhabitants – more than one third of the total population – had been urbanized: forced either into towns or special centres, a euphemism for what were in effect concentration camps. Hundreds of thousands of peasants were scratching the most precarious of livings from the soil; some 60,000 had no work at all. Tens of thousands of draught buffalo and oxen had been killed. In the towns of the province also the end of the war had brought economic chaos. Many of their people had formerly been employed by the numerous agencies spawned by the war; new sources of livelihood for them had yet to be found.[8]

There was an immediate threat of famine. The US-backed Saigon regime had been able to import 30,000 tons of rice each year for Nghia Binh. When, with the end of the war, that source of supply dried up, relief supplies were sent from the North and from other provinces in the South. However, the new government could not continue such provision indefinitely. The authorities in Nghia Binh resolved to make the province self-sufficient in food within a year, no matter what the cost in effort and in self-denial. At the same time they had to cope with other, hardly less urgent, problems. Diseases, proliferated by decades of continuous warfare, had to be eradicated. Social evils, exacerbated by harsh economic conditions, flared up – burglaries, robberies, street fights and murders. Fanning the flames were remnants of the previous administration and its army who had evaded registration and gone into hiding. According to the Communists, agents of the old regime were busy 'propagating their distorting and vilifying allegations against the revolution in an attempt to confuse and bewilder the population and make things as difficult as possible for the newly established power'.[9]

The 'newly established power' was seriously hampered in the South by a lack of experienced cadres, many of whom had been killed in the course of the 1968 Tet Offensive and the CIA's Phoenix Programme whereby PRG suspects, as well as many others who had no connection with revolutionary movements, were tracked down and liquidated.[10] Furthermore, deprived of the services of those who had shown most zeal and commitment, it had to contend with disruption caused by the very people who had eliminated the cadres. Frank Snepp, the CIA's main strategy analyst at the time in Vietnam, has pointed out that among those left behind by the Americans when they withdrew were 'countless counter terrorist agents – perhaps numbering as high as 30,000 – specially trained to operate with the Phoenix programme'.[11]

How to neutralize such people and how to integrate the many other Vietnamese who had comprised the old governing system was one of the new regime's major tasks. Opponents of the Communists had for years terrified the South Vietnamese with warnings that a blood-bath would undoubtedly follow a Communist victory. Thus Patrick Honey predicted: 'All believed to pose a threat, real or potential, to the Communist regime will be killed at once, and some of the remainder may be permitted to postpone execution as long as they continue to work as unpaid slave labourers. Calculated on the basis of past Communist deeds, and given the size of South Vietnam's population, the minimum number of those to be butchered will exceed one million and could rise to several times that figure.'[12] Horror stories such as this were peddled continually and widely believed. They provoked, in the spring of 1975, an hysterical flight by those who were able to escape and loaded those forced to remain with a sense of impending doom. In the event, the people of South Vietnam were soon disabused, as the new power established itself with a minimal use of force. A Western journalist reported in May 1975:

> The possibility that the panicky mass evacuation of Vietnam was unnecessary has added yet another humiliation to the American defeat in Vietnam. It certainly indicates once again a failure to understand the Vietnamese and this particular Asian communism. As the second week of communist rule in South Vietnam drew to an end, this correspondent was questioned by several Vietnamese on how it might be possible to bring back families that had been sent to the United States at the urging of 'American friends'.[13]

In fact there was no blood-bath either in the first fortnight of the new regime or later.

The policy of the new rulers was indeed to put an end to internal conflict, not to foment it, despite the dreadful record of tortures and murders committed under the previous government. How that record was discounted is illustrated by the response of a Communist cadre, when he was asked how he could pardon a policeman who had tortured his wife to death: 'It is very simple to understand. You have to go back to the origin of the problem. It was the Americans who forced people to commit all those crimes. Basically, we are all victims of American imperialism. We have to understand this and forgive our brothers.' His questioner reported that the cadre's manner was sincere and that his statement did not sound like a propaganda lecture.[14]

Apart from any question of morality, it was not in the interest of the new government to deal harshly with its former enemies. The prime minister of the PRG, Huyn Tan Phat, explained their attitude in October 1975: 'If we had used force we would not have been able to rally people to our side. Our fundamental policy was that of peace and national concord. That is why we decided on a step-by-step approach in dealing with the enemy, causing division in their ranks, isolating the most reactionary elements.'[15]

Their approach involved the re-education of people in South Vietnam who had been for years under the thumb of those who viewed the revolutionaries as bloodthirsty monsters. For many citizens this took the form of meetings at which the revolutionary message was regularly and relentlessly reiterated. For officials of the old regime it usually entailed compulsory detention in re-education and work camps. The regimen in those camps was a mixture of lectures, study sessions and other activities focused on getting people to renounce their reactionary ideas, together with compulsory manual labour – constructing dykes, clearing land and in other ways helping the post-war reconstruction. Many of the detainees were released within a few days or weeks and their civil rights restored if they did not participate in counter-revolutionary activities. Executives and managerial personnel of the old regime and of anti-revolutionary political parties were, after release, kept under surveillance for periods of six months to one year before having their civil rights restored.

Those who proved recalcitrant – refusing to follow the regulations or taking part in rebellious activities – were detained for a total of three years re-education and labour: a sentence subject to reduction if they worked well. Those responsible for crimes against the people were brought to trial and punished if found guilty. The government reported that by April 1976 95 per cent of those detained had been freed from all surveillance and had taken part in the elections for a reunified Vietnam. Pham Van Dong, the prime minister of the reunited country, stated in April 1977 that almost all detainees had been released, with a small number of 'diehard counter-revolutionaries remaining in detention for some more time'.[16]

The elections, in which the great majority of soldiers and officials of the old government participated, were held on 25 April 1976. Thus, twenty years after the time fixed at Geneva, a single National Assembly for the whole of Vietnam was elected, on the basis of one deputy for each 100,000 of population. The deputies, 249 from the North and 243 from the South, met for their first session on 24 June and on 2 July the reunification was formally declared. The new Socialist Republic of Vietnam had as its capital Hanoi, the city which for so long had been the heart of resistance to the foreigner; its first leader, as already noted, was Pham Van Dong, previously prime minister of North Vietnam.

Some observers commented unfavourably on the take-over, as they saw it, of the southern half of the country by hard-faced men from North Vietnam. Immediately after the Spring Victory one knowledgeable journalist had pointed out the advantage to the country of maintaining a distinct role for the PRG in South Vietnam. 'While continuing to work for reunification,' he wrote, 'the PRG as a separate entity is likely to benefit from worldwide goodwill, including that of Western countries which have stopped toeing the American line towards Vietnam. By pursuing a policy of neutrality and independence the PRG is also likely to carve a leading role in the increasingly powerful Third World bloc, something which would not be possible by formally joining the socialist bloc.'[17] However, writing a year later, the same journalist recognized the difficulties that had been caused by the lack in the South of experienced cadres.[18] To remedy that it was only sensible to deploy administrative talent where it was needed even if that policy gave a preponderant role to cadres and officials from the North. Furthermore, the idea that a quasi-independent PRG might evoke foreign sympathy proved illusory. The fact was that in the year following the fall of Saigon there had been scant evidence of any international goodwill towards either the PRG or the people and government of North Vietnam.

There was no inducement to perpetuate a separate identity for a government in the South for the sake of influencing a few foreign friends who proved to be non-existent. Indeed as it became clear that the Vietnamese would have to rely on their own enthusiasm and talents, the early reunification of the country became an even greater priority. Obviously the new Vietnam would be socialist; thanks to the policies followed by the United States and their clients, no force other than the Communists had any claim to govern the country. A new socialist country could be achieved only by fully integrating both its parts. Even more fundamental than political pressures was the powerful pull of Vietnamese history. Much of that history was a record of Vietnamese struggle to preserve a national identity despite foreign incursions. 'Nothing is more precious than independence and freedom': Ho Chi Minh's slogan, which had sustained the Vietnamese during the war, pointed, after the war was over, to reunification.

.During the year preceding reunification much had been achieved in helping North and South to recover from the effect of the war. There had been considerable success in rehabilitating some of its casualties: the orphans were being cared for, the prostitutes retrained for other work, and drug addicts were being treated by a combination of methods – re-education, acupuncture, traditional methods and sedatives. Many industrial installations in the North that were destroyed during the war had been rebuilt. In the South, the industrial sector had, owing to the rapidity of the Saigon government's collapse, remained almost intact and a number of high-capacity installations were equipped with modern machinery.

Some progress had been made also in tackling one of the most urgent problems in the South – the resettlement of those peasants who had been forced off the land and had been barely surviving either in overcrowded camps or in wretched slums in the towns and cities. The government's solution had been to establish 'new economic zones'. These were areas of hitherto unusable land which were to be cleared and brought under cultivation by people from the overcrowded cities. Work in the zones also formed part of the programme of re-education and training for the more high-ranking and recalcitrant officials of the Saigon regime.

The new economic zones have been described as hell-holes, established by the Communists to punish their enemies and to impose a harsh life on the inhabitants of cities in the South. However, the weight of the evidence indicates that the new government, far from seeking to punish its former enemies, was anxious to enrol as many as possible in the work of reconstruction. Earl Martin, an American Mennonite who observed the early days of the Communist regime, has written that 'the fact that the revolutionary government had clearly delineated the policy of "reeducation" exercises at all may well have been a primary factor for the virtual lack of personal recriminations and blood-letting after the change of government. If no clear program had been outlined, the bitter enmity accumulated over the years would possibly have resulted in a far uglier spectacle at the war's end.'[19] This chimes with the remark of a PRG official: 'We have educated our people to abstain from revenge. We have made so many sacrifices in the past 30 years that the sacrifice of abstaining from revenge is small in comparison. Especially when the prize is national reconciliation. We draw a line under the past.'[20]

It was in fact essential to reclaim land to feed the fast-growing population of Vietnam and to find work for peasants who had been detached from their livelihood by a deliberate bombing campaign. What else could be done to produce both crops and work and to compensate for food supplies from abroad which were cut off when the Saigon government fell? The work was certainly hard, the conditions of life austere and the government could supply little in the way of agricultural machinery to make the job easier. It is hardly surprising that many of those working in the zones felt exposed to hardship. On the other hand there were also many, especially among the young, who met the challenge with enthusiasm and dedication.[21]

The re-education of former enemies, rehabilitation of the casualties of war and the settling of the new economic zones were some of the immediate tasks of the new administration. It also appreciated that a longer-term strategy had to be worked out. The ultimate objective was to have Vietnam functioning as a truly socialist state; many obstacles, however, stood in the way. The country was underdeveloped and had a weak base on which to build an industrialized economy. It had a rapidly increasing population, a heavy load of foreign indebtedness, and was not receiving adequate aid and credits either from Communist or from Western sources. Furthermore, the job of overcoming those impediments had to be tackled sooner than was expected: the new leaders, like other Vietnamese, were surprised by the speed of their own forces.

Contrary to the impression generally given in Western media, they faced their problems in a flexible and non-doctrinaire way. In the first few months after their victory, the PRG in the South had, for example, sought the co-operation of those identified as national capitalists, as contrasted with compradore-capitalists – those who had worked hand-in-glove with foreign companies. A decree of September 1975 indicated that the PRG would encourage and help national capitalists, small enterprises, handicrafts and small merchants to develop industry and trade which would be profitable to themselves and would also serve the national economy. From Hanoi, Pham Van Dong invited national capitalists who had formerly been held back by foreign competitors to 'put all their talents and ardour at the great cause of the nation', now that it was free and independent.[22]

This readiness to seek support from beyond the ranks of the Communist Party was still in evidence after reunification. Within a year of the founding of the new Socialist Republic, observers noted that the Vietnamese leaders were prepared to devote the next twenty years to the implementing of a 'new economic policy'. They saw this as a tactically necessary stage during which private, domestic and foreign capital would be used to realize the country's agricultural and industrial potential. It appeared that they were confident they could remain essentially true to their socialist goals while utilizing Western capital, technology and even management techniques to attain them. Officials of the International Monetary Fund, having visited Vietnam in November 1976, reported that there was 'sufficient ground for moderate optimism' regarding the financial policy being followed by Hanoi.[23]

By the time of the thirty-second anniversary of Ho Chi Minh's declaration of Vietnamese independence – in September 1945 – the country seemed to be making a slow but satisfactory recovery from the long wars that had followed his defiant gesture. That was certainly the picture emerging from an article, 'Dong's quiet anniversary', written by Nayan Chanda in September 1977. With reference to some of the pressing social problems he stated:

> Thanks to a campaign for adult education and community schooling for children the literacy rate has risen appreciably. Notwithstanding shortage of equipment and medicine, a cleanliness and vaccination drive has prevented major epidemics. International agency officials say that they are impressed by the purposefulness and devotion with which a rudimentary health service has been set up in the south. Although woefully

inadequate for the enormity of the task, the rehabilitation centres for prostitutes and drug addicts have helped several thousand people find a normal life.

Commenting on the economy, Chanda observed that within less than two years of reunification a well-balanced and realistic economic development plan had been drawn up. Vietnam had joined the International Monetary Fund, the World Bank and the Asian Development Bank and had sought bilateral assistance in order to finance its economic plan. Domestic resources had been mobilized to expand the acreage under food and cash crops, to dig canals and to build dykes and reservoirs. Despite a shortage of draught animals and tools more than a hundred new economic zones had been established to provide 'a productive, if harsh and rudimentary life to thousands of jobless families from Saigon'. The country's dislocated network of communications had been largely repaired and the railway link between Hanoi and Saigon had been restored. Although the 1976 export level of US $206 million represented only a modest 2 per cent increase over the previous year, exports from the North had increased by 15 per cent.[24]

However, even as this article was being written, tensions in Vietnam's foreign relations were also increasing and were to lead to international ostracism of the Hanoi government and to a critical accentuation of its economic and social problems.

Twelve

NEW WARS AND NEW PROBLEMS

The foreign policy of the new Vietnam was aimed at 'upholding the banner of national independence and socialism'. To achieve that aim its leaders were ready to work together with other countries and organizations whose objectives were very different from their own. A Canadian observer who met prominent members of the government in November 1976 remarked that their decision to join the World Bank and the IMF, to seek foreign investments in oil, mining and metallurgical projects from Western Europe, Japan and Canada, as well as from the Soviet Union, together with their grateful acceptance of aid from the Scandinavian countries – all showed their desire for flexibility in foreign affairs.[1] Regarding their neighbours in Southeast Asia, they indicated a wish to establish 'good neighbourly relations, economic co-operation and cultural exchange to mutual benefit'. All countries in the region should respect each others' 'independence, sovereignty and territorial integrity'.[2] Since the Vietnamese were faced with such a mammoth task of reconstruction and had so few resources of their own, it was imperative that they avoid further conflict and foster international goodwill towards themselves.

Two major powers, China and the United States, were not, however, prepared to respond to any overtures from the Vietnamese. Since the Vietnam War had been felt by so many influential Americans to be an appalling humiliation, it is no wonder that their government used its vast economic and diplomatic strength to isolate and weaken its former antagonist. In 1973 the United States had been a signatory to the Paris Agreement which included the following statement: 'In pursuance of its traditional policy, the United States will contribute to healing the wounds of war and to postwar reconstruction of the Democratic Republic of Vietnam and throughout Indochina.'[3] President Nixon, it appeared, had promised $3.25 billion of economic assistance, spread over a period of five years and without any political conditions attached. However, in 1975, President Ford and Henry Kissinger, his Secretary of State, proposed a total trade embargo,

21. President Nixon with Chou En-lai on his visit to China in 1972.

refused to discuss reconstruction aid or normalization of relations and blocked Vietnam's bid for a seat in the United Nations.[4] Their policy on these matters was followed also by President Carter who, when asked whether the United States had 'a moral obligation to help to rebuild Vietnam', denied that any debt was owed, on the grounds that 'the destruction was mutual'![5] In 1978, a year after that remarkable statement, the Vietnamese, in increasing economic difficulties, showed themselves willing to discuss, without preconditions, the normalization of relations with the Americans. Carter's government not only rebuffed them but also voted against the Asian Development Bank's allocating funds to Vietnam.[6]

Those actions were consistent with the policy of American governments since the early 1950s of combating revolutionary nationalism in Vietnam. On the other hand, the growing hostility shown by the rulers of Communist China to their southern neighbour indicated a significant shift of attitude. Since its founding in 1949, Red China had been one of the principal enemies of the United States. It had sent substantial aid to the Vietnamese when they were fighting the Americans. However, during the course of that war the Chinese leaders became increasingly convinced that their security was threatened more by the Soviet Union than by the United States. The reasons for the Sino-Soviet split, which had been growing ever wider since the early 1960s, cannot be explored in this context. We can, however, register the readiness of the Chinese and the Americans to submerge their differences for the sake of counteracting Soviet influence, both in the world generally and especially in East Asia. From 1972, when, at the height of the Vietnam War, Nixon was fêted in Peking, there was a growing rapprochement between the People's Republic and the United States. According to Banning Garrett (an American expert with access to sources in the Pentagon, the CIA, the State Department and the National Security Council), the US military relationship with China, which had developed substantially by the late 1970s, was 'the outcome of studies and plans made by the Pentagon since 1973'.[7] Those developments naturally disenchanted the hard-pressed Vietnamese, as did the Chinese occupation in 1974 of the Paracel Islands, which the Vietnamese claimed as their own; to forestall any additional annexation by China, they made a point, in the following year, of liberating the Spratly Islands from the Saigon regime.[8] Thus by 1975 relations between China and Vietnam were already strained. They became increasingly embittered as a result of Chinese support of the Khmer Rouge regime which assumed control of Cambodia on 17 April 1975.

From 1970 to 1975 the Khmer Rouge and the Vietnamese Communists had both been struggling to destroy US puppet regimes. While there had been, in the past, some disagreements between the two factions, it was not unreasonable to expect that, having defeated the forces of reaction, they would collaborate with each other in creating socialist societies in their respective countries. In fact, there was immediate antipathy between them, the causes of which appear to be both ideological and historical.

The differences in their ideas about how to establish a socialist order are seen most clearly in their distinct ways of tackling the problem of urbanization. As we have noted, the Vietnamese authorities, while establishing new economic zones, tolerated many divergencies from a strict socialist path, in order not to antagonize those people in the south who had been accustomed to a way of life created by the preponderant influence there, for many years, of the United States. In the view of one observer: 'For almost three years the capitalist heart of southern Vietnam remained largely untouched by the country's new communist rulers.'[9] Pol Pot, the leader of the Khmer Rouge, adopted a drastically different policy in Kampuchea, as Cambodia was renamed, according to the constitution which came into force in 1975. He was in no mood to compromise. The inhabitants of the capital, Phnom Penh, and other cities and towns, were abruptly expelled and forced to work alongside the peasants in the country-side. All traces of capitalism, including the use of money as a means of exchange, were obliterated. Everywhere the transition to social-ism was swift and brutal.[10]

While the Vietnamese disappointed their enemies by substi-tuting re-education and rehabilitation for the oft-promised but never-realized blood-bath, the Khmer Rouge did not hesitate to carry out mass executions of its opponents. Whether the victims numbered thousands or millions is a matter of sad dispute. There is no question, however, that the tactics employed by Pol Pot were widely at variance with the methods of Pham Van Dong and his colleagues. In Vietnam and in Kampuchea the roads to socialism were indeed very different.

As significant as the ideological split between the two countries was the deep-rooted mutual suspicion that was a product of their history. Milton Osborne has pointed out that 'the Pol Pot govern-ment's policy towards Vietnam fitted firmly into a long tradition of fundamental ethnic antipathy and distrust between Vietnam and Cambodia'. In support of that view, he cites events in the

1830s, when the Vietnamese occupied much of Cambodia and sought to 'remake Cambodia and its population into a pale imitation of Vietnam'. The Khmer Rouge were, he argues, convinced that the Vietnamese Communists were intent on dominating all the countries of the former French Indochina, thus 'adding a contemporary slant to an age-old Vietnamese plan'.[11] We have commented above that in 1975 the Vietnamese had enough to do in the rebuilding of their own country without seeking to take over their neighbour. Even so, Pol Pot was evidently concerned that they were a threat to Kampuchea and launched attacks on them across the border.

After a series of incidents both sides agreed to have talks in May 1976 but were unable to settle their differences. Following a number of serious encounters dating from April 1977, the Vietnamese responded forcefully in September then undertook a major offensive in December. Having carried out punitive raids in Kampuchea they subsequently withdrew and in February 1978 offered peace terms to the Khmer Rouge. They were, they claimed, ready to negotiate a peaceful settlement of any border dispute and to allow international supervision of an agreed frontier. The Kampucheans ignored this overture and the conflict continued. Although the Vietnamese had an undoubted military superiority they were unwilling to push a full-scale invasion. Such a move, they feared, might provoke a direct reaction from China and might also 'seriously tarnish Vietnam's international image and hamper its aid-raising efforts'.[12]

However, in December 1978, Vietnamese troops did invade Kampuchea. On 7 January 1979 Phnom Penh was captured by Vietnamese-backed rebels and on the following day a People's Revolutionary Committee under Heng Samrin replaced the Khmer Rouge as the government. Differing explanations have been offered for this change of policy. Nayan Chanda has attributed it to a feeling in Hanoi that 'it was this dry season or never'. The Vietnamese, he believed, were worried that Kampuchea, after nearly two years of isolation, was slowly opening its doors and trying to improve an international image which had been rendered odious by Khmer Rouge excesses. They feared that Pol Pot might have done enough to 'make any Vietnamese drive difficult if not impossible' and so decided to risk suffering the consequences that previously had deterred them.[13]

A different interpretation, more sympathetic to the Vietnamese, has claimed that Hanoi was forced to mount a defensive operation 'related to the same issue which had obsessively concerned them for a generation: the unification of Vietnam'. A protracted conflict on the Kampuchean border threatened the whole process of peaceful unification and the integrity of the revolution in the South. By the end of 1978 half a million hectares of land that had been cleared were once again lying fallow. To combat the after-effects of defoliation it was essential to get them under cultivation; however, that was not possible while there was fighting 'which displaced hundreds of thousands of peasants and obliged even more extremely fertile ricelands to be left untouched, except by shells'. According to this argument, Hanoi could not have tolerated a long war 'along its socially fractious and economically fertile Cambodian border. A war in the remoter regions of the Cardamom Mountains was obviously preferable.... Thus Vietnam, to strike back *in its own defence* had to do the job completely.'[14]

An official Vietnamese version states that they were acting in self-defence and in support of opponents of the Khmer Rouge who had organized themselves into a National United Front for the Salvation of Kampuchea. One of its leaders was Heng Samrin who, as we have seen, came to power in the wake of the Vietnamese army and who, according to Hanoi, had begun to resist Pol Pot when he realized that his country was being led 'straight into total extermination'.[15]

It may be noted, in this context, that the Vietnamese, as a result of events in China, Pol Pot's principal ally, had cause to be concerned about their own survival. In May 1978, Brzezinski, President Carter's adviser on national security, visited Peking: during his visit the Chinese claimed that Vietnam was playing in Southeast Asia the role taken by Cuba in Africa; it was being manipulated by the Soviet Union to undermine stability in the region.[16] According to some observers, Chinese open hostility to Vietnam dates from that visit. In August, China closed its border with Vietnam and during the next few months there was growing tension between the two communist neighbours. No doubt these developments encouraged the Vietnamese to strike, as they hoped, decisively against Kampuchea, with the intention, in part, of avoiding conflict simultaneously on two fronts.

The countries who comprised the Association of South East Asian Nations – Malaysia, Singapore, Thailand, Indonesia and the Philippines – certainly did not consider the Vietnamese attack on Kampuchea as a defensive response to external threats. For them, as for most other countries, it was a definite act of aggression: evidence that Vietnam was intent on establishing its hegemony over the whole of Indochina.[17] To some powers, notably the Chinese and the Americans, it signalled an unwelcome increase in Soviet influence in the area. In June 1978 Vietnam had joined Comecon, the Council for Mutual Economic Assistance, which was dominated by the Soviet Union. The fact that the Vietnamese had been obliged to seek closer co-operation with Moscow because US pressure had ensured that no other country would offer them sufficient economic aid was ignored; as was the fact that Vietnam had no intention of becoming a Soviet satellite.

The hostility shown to Vietnam by most other members of the international community was intensified as a result of their considerable agitation concerning its refugees. In January 1979 an editorial in the *Far Eastern Economic Review* included the following condemnation:

> The Stalinist hardliners who have won political ascendancy over the liberals in the Hanoi government are worse than hooligans. The policies of intolerance they have adopted over the past year are creating a society so loathsome that hundreds of thousands of Vietnamese citizens – ethnic Chinese and Vietnamese alike – would rather commit themselves to the seas in leaky junks ... and trust in the sour charity of neighbouring countries than face the future in their own homes.[18]

During the summer of 1979 that judgement seemed confirmed by the fact that the 'boat people' were arriving in other Southeast Asian countries at the rate of over 50,000 a month.

The situation was not, however, so clear-cut as it was usually presented in the mass media. Helen Steven reported in *The Guardian*:

> Most of the boat people ... do not give directly political reasons for fleeing and could be classed as economic refugees. Many are middle-class professionals or owners of small businesses, and many, if not directly working for the Americans, benefited

from the inflated US salaries and life-style.... Vietnam is no longer a consumer society, partly owing to desperate economic stringencies, partly because of the revolution.... Economic social pressures have forced small traders out of business.... To families seeing their life-savings dwindling, a new life in California, Australia or Britain seems a last hope.... The Vietnam government offers the alternative of working on the land in the new economic zones. Tools, material for a house, seeds and transport are made available. Some have accepted and even welcome the offer ... but to a family accustomed to an urban Western life-style, it is hard to labour unremittingly on the land, often without electricity or running water.

She went on to emphasize the contrast between 'the corrupt, materialist, sophisticated Saigon' and the 'self-discipline and dedication of Hanoi'. In North Vietnam, she noted, 'deprivation is accepted as part of a patriotic struggle for which huge sacrifices are made. In the South hard times are accepted with resentment.'[19]

Many of those who were most resentful were the Hoa – people of Chinese descent who, in the first quarter of 1978, 'were mainly responsible for the success of a growing black market, not merely in the South but also in North Vietnam – a market which had cornered the bulk of the rice supply'.[20] Not surprisingly, the Vietnamese government first closed down more than 30,000 private businesses in Cholon, the predominantly Chinese twin city of Saigon, then introduced a new currency in order to eliminate cash hoarding. To describe those actions as 'policies of intolerance' is a reflection more of the bias of Western opinion than of the true intention of those dismissed as 'Stalinist hardliners'.

For the most part, the critics of the Vietnamese government represented the exodus of refugees as a consequence of political repression and ignored the highly relevant economic factors. Some of those factors were included in a report compiled in the autumn of 1978 by the League of the Red Cross. It pointed out that recently 4 million people had been affected by severe flooding in Vietnam, at least half of whom would need emergency relief for the next six months. The immediate result of the floods had been the destruction of 10,000 head of cattle, of 32,000 pigs, of 200,000 poultry as well as 50 health clinics, 1,000 classrooms and 1,000 small factories. Officials in Ho Chi Minh City had calculated that more than 80 per cent of the winter rice crop had been ruined. Even before the flooding, crops in the Mekong Delta had been destroyed by a plague of brown planthoppers which had resulted from a lack of pesticides and of spare parts for plant sprayers. Those catastrophes had exacerbated an already desperate situation, whereby in 1977 there had been a food gap of 1.6 million tons.[21]

These facts indicate the harshness of life in Vietnam and help to explain why so many people who, in any case, did not support the aims of the government, were anxious to flee – particularly those who had enjoyed a privileged status at the time of the puppet regime. Given the many other problems facing it, the government, not unnaturally, was not inclined to use scarce resources to smooth the way for the refugees. In their view, the refugee problem was largely a consequence of US involvement in Vietnamese affairs. They recalled that in 1975 the Americans themselves had evacuated many Vietnamese who they thought would be at risk under Communist rule. In July 1979, the Vietnamese Foreign Minister pointed out that while the Americans were demanding liberty of emigration for the refugees, they would not allow them access to the United States itself. He wondered why the United States should not, as previously, organize airlifts and use its Seventh Fleet to remove those who wished to settle in the West. There was some sympathy among the ASEAN countries for the Vietnamese attitude, with one Malaysian newspaper describing the boat problem as 'a hangover of US involvement in South Vietnam'.[22]

More usually, however, ASEAN leaders were highly critical of the Vietnamese and described the flood of refugees as 'a Hanoi-designed operation' to destabilize the whole region.[23] They indicated that they would not take any more into their countries: at one point the authorities in Malaysia even threatened to shoot boat people who tried to land in future.[24] They also accused the Vietnamese regime of profiteering from the crisis by extorting gold from the boat people. Nguyen Co Thach, the Foreign Minister, admitted that some lower officials had been corrupt but denied any concerted policy of extortion. He also promised that the guilty would be punished and observed that the very fact that refugees had made gold payments indicated that they were not being forced out, as had been alleged, but were leaving voluntarily.[25]

While defending its own position, the Hanoi government accepted, nevertheless, the need to respond to intense international pressure and during the summer of 1979 collaborated with the UN High Commission for Refugees in arranging a more orderly emigration. In August a Western correspondent was able to record that 'the fever has eased – ships have picked up a few hundred boat people in the weeks following the Geneva conference, but none apparently have had to pay to leave and the number of Vietnamese in camps throughout Southeast Asia has stopped multiplying'. She anticipated that refugee camps in the region would be cleared by the end of 1980.[26]

As suggested above, comment by Western media on the refugee question was, in the main, partisan and misleading. Chomsky and Herman have observed: 'The treatment of refugees in the mass media and by US official action seems to depend, once again, on political–economic–ideological, rather than human rights considerations.' Having enumerated the very large numbers of people fleeing from Burma and from parts of Latin America, contemporaneously with the movements from Indochina, they contrast the responses to the different categories of refugees. Regarding those from Burma: 'no one cares'; in Latin America: 'the flow stems from actions serviceable to US interests'; in Indochina: 'the blame can be placed on the evils of Communism – overlooking the insignificant matter of the legacy of US intervention'. Accordingly:

> Refugees of the first and second categories can be shipped back to tyranny or left to rot in oblivion wherever they may land (as long as it is not here). But refugees of the third category call forth stirring cries of indignation, editorial denunciation, passionate speeches in the halls of Congress, outraged protest from spokesmen for human rights, and moving words – rarely deeds – of compassion in keeping with the lofty traditions of Western humanism.[27]

While there was unremitting publicity about the fate of the boat people who hoped to settle in the West, comparatively little attention was paid to another exodus which was of much greater import for Vietnam itself. Between April 1978 and the summer of 1979 some 250,000 Hoa, mostly from North Vietnam, fled into China. Hanoi's accusation that this mass movement was the result of a deliberate scare campaign mounted by Peking, was corroborated by Wilfred Burchett in a report in *The Guardian*:

> In three visits to the northern frontier areas in December 1978 and April–May 1979, and in innumerable conversations with Hoa residents of Hanoi, Haiphong and Ho Chi Minh City, I found ample proof of pressures on ethnic Chinese to flee Vietnam ... the propaganda patter of Chinese agents was: 'Vietnam is at war with Kampuchea. We support Kampuchea, the Soviet Union supports Vietnam. War between China and Vietnam is inevitable. If you remain, the Vietnamese will treat you as enemies, our troops will deal with you as traitors'.[28]

The war between China and Vietnam in fact broke out in February 1979 when the Chinese invaded in force across the frontier. Both sides suffered considerable casualties and on Vietnamese territory several towns and many villages were destroyed. However, the conflict was short-lived: at the beginning of March the Chinese withdrew their troops and an uneasy peace ensued. Several reasons have been advanced for the Chinese taking the offensive when they did.[29] It is claimed that they wished to teach the Vietnamese a lesson; to show that 'they could not be pushed around'; to 'destroy the myth of Vietnamese invincibility' and also to offer some respite to the Khmer Rouge who were being hard-pressed by the Vietnamese and their allies in Kampuchea.

In the event, their attack on Vietnam achieved no decisive result. Nevertheless, Hanoi was left with no illusions about the continuing threat from Peking. Shortly after the Chinese withdrawal, Nayan Chanda observed that while Vietnam's ability to provoke internal disorder in China was limited, the Chinese could at little cost 'encourage opposition to the Hanoi regime by diverse elements, thus stretching its armed forces and draining its resources'.[30] Even in August 1978 he had noted that one of the serious long-term consequences of Vietnam's conflicts with both China and Pol Pot was its drafting of more men into the army and the self-defence force. Not only did that prevent their use for other productive work but, additionally, the new drive to strengthen Vietnam's defences was interrupting the work done in agriculture and in road and bridge building by the army, as well as the fishing duties undertaken in more normal times by the navy.[31]

During 1979 the continuing embroilment with China, the need to maintain a large army in Kampuchea and the results of international ostracism were all contributing to the breakdown of the Vietnamese economy. Although it was aware of the consequences, the government could not risk relaxing its military effort. Withdrawal of its support for Heng Samrin, for example, might result in the emergence of an independent Kampuchea, no doubt inimical to Vietnam, which 'enjoying massive international assistance and prospering under a capitalist system would have serious repercussions on the still unruly and hard-to-manage south'. Thus, at the beginning of 1980, the Vietnamese had little option other than to 'tighten their belts and grit their teeth for a few more years', in the hope that a pro-Vietnamese regime in Kampuchea would ultimately be tolerated by the international community and that, with Soviet help, the economy would stage a recovery.[32]

In August 1980 yet another series of typhoons, the third in three successive years, hit Vietnam, thus forcing the Vietnamese to tighten their belts even more as grain supplies were further depleted. One official, amazed at his compatriots' capacity for endurance, claimed that, amidst such hardship and suffering, 'in any other country, the government would have been changed'. He conceded, however, that there was no choice other than to support the government in resisting the Chinese, if Vietnam were to remain independent.[33]

Even for that cause, many Vietnamese were finding it hard to tolerate such hardships. As the economic crisis deepened corruption became a problem even among party cadres. In September 1980, the prime minister, Pham Van Dong, promised to ensure the effective rationing of food and to stabilize prices while, at the same time, attacking acts of embezzlement and illegal transactions by some officials. Shortly afterwards *Nhan Dan*, the party newspaper, warned that the enemy was taking advantage of the country's difficulties to sow misgiving and uncertainty in the ranks of the people and complained that 'not a few comrades have let down their guard in the face of the enemy's cunning scheme'.[34] By the end of the year there was additional evidence of discontent. Theft and burglary increased, anti-government graffiti appeared on walls in Hanoi and there were food riots in Haiphong and in Nghe Tinh province. Malnutrition resulting from food shortages led to a fall in productivity and there was general demoralization and lassitude. One official declared: 'The stomach is our principal concern.'[35] The Vice Premier sadly predicted: 'We will be poor and we will be hungry until the end of this century.'[36]

Accentuating the problems caused by the lack of food was the rapid growth in population. In 1975 it was estimated to be 47 million. The first 'all national population census' in 1979 revealed an increase to nearly 53 million and it was expected that an additional million would be added by mid-1980. If the trend were to continue unchecked the population, by the year 2000, would be 100 million.[37]

The Vietnamese leaders realized that, in addition to population control, other measures were needed urgently to halt the collapse of the economy and stem the growing disaffection. Even in 1979 there had in fact been a liberalization of the regulations governing private enterprise which allowed greater freedom to private producers both in agriculture and in industry. Within a year more than 2,000 small family enterprises had sprung up in Ho Chi Minh City. During the same period, certain state-run industrial and fishing concerns introduced piece-rate wages instead of fixed monthly salaries. Consequently, in one state-owned fishing company, the catch in 1980 was more than double the figure for 1979 – 15,000 tons instead of 7,061 tons.[38]

By a decree of October 1980, the government sought to stabilize, for a period of five years, both the grain tax and the arrangements for the purchase of agricultural products. Thus, up to 1985, co-operatives and individual peasants would be expected to pay 10 per cent on average of the volume of their grain as tax. The amount of their produce they must sell to the state would be decided on the basis of average yield and the volume of production in the previous five years.

Producers were to know in advance how much they were required to sell at the fixed price: any surplus could be sold at an agreed higher price, either to the state or to the free market. The intention was to steer a middle course between rigid planning and unrestrained private initiative. In so doing the government hoped to maintain a minimum standard of living by selling essential goods at a low price while encouraging productivity through the offer of a higher buying price, to agricultural producers, for goods bought above the quota.

There was some doubt as to whether such a dual price policy was realistic, in view of the low productivity of light industry and the resultant drastic shortage of consumer goods. Some observers noted that so long as the government failed to supply essential goods to the peasants, higher cash prices for farm products would not remove basic imbalances from the economy. To break the continuing cycle of underdevelopment and falling growth, a big injection was required of agricultural inputs and consumer goods. However, such an injection was hardly to be expected from the Soviet Union and there seemed to be no other possible source.[39]

At the beginning of 1981, Nguyen Lam, Vice Premier and Chairman of the State Planning Commission, outlined the government's attitude to the crisis. Referring to the huge military expenditure, he commented: 'If there was no threat of war, I could have concentrated on the economy. But I don't know when that will happen.' He did know that, in the next five years, 6 million more people would enter the job market. It would be necessary to persuade them to work in agriculture, to go to the new economic zones or to engage in handicrafts. The government would also have to intensify family planning to reduce the annual population growth to 2.2 per cent in the next five years. As to those who were already in work, he recognized the need to increase the salaries of some 3.5 million state employees and workers, without, however, specifying how the money was to be made available.

Regarding foreign trade, he admitted that imports from non-communist countries were negligible because the Vietnamese could not pay for them. Nor could they afford to import raw materials, which previously had come from capitalist countries, for their consumer industry. Thus to fill the gap in consumer provision they had to promote small industries and handicrafts. On the question of management, he pointed out that the government was launching a strong anti-bureaucratic campaign which, he claimed, was being welcomed by the majority of people.[40] In this he was echoing a point made by the party stalwart, Le Duan, that in the recent past the party and the state had 'committed the greatest shortcomings and mistakes primarily in economic planning and in the domain of distribution and circulation of goods'. To avoid further mismanagement it was necessary, as Duan put it, to perfect the state organs from central echelons to the grassroots levels. He warned that without such a reform no economic policy could be carried out thoroughly.[41]

To conclude this brief review of the economy we may note that the government's proposals for economic changes were discussed with a team from the International Monetary Fund which visited Hanoi late in 1980. The team advised the government that it could aim for a higher inflation rate in order to give a boost to the sagging economy. As an additional stimulus, the IMF offered Vietnam US $36.9 million in loans for the year up to September 1981.[42]

What then was the state of Vietnam at the end of 1980? As to its foreign policy, the Hanoi government was continuing to maintain a large army in Kampuchea in order to preserve the Heng Samrin regime against the persistent attacks of the reconstituted Khmer Rouge and other Chinese-backed factions, including a number of right-wing groups. Against intense international pressure, they contended that any withdrawal from Kampuchea would place their own national security in jeopardy. In part, their intransigence over Kampuchea was determined by their fear of the Washington–Peking axis. We have already noted some of the earlier contacts between the United States and China in the 1970s. In 1978 they both agreed on full diplomatic normalization and in the following year the Chinese leader, Deng Xiaoping, returned the visits made to China by Nixon and Ford when he himself visited the United States.

The common hostility of both powers towards Vietnam drew them ever closer. Early in 1980, Harold Brown, Carter's Defense Secretary, admitted that Washington had 'done quite a lot in terms of urging others ... to impose economic penalties on Vietnam'. Noting that the United States and China saw eye to eye on Afghanistan and Kampuchea, he stated that the present task was 'to ensure that our converging assessments are translated into effective responses'.[43] Later in that year an official of the State Department expounded the same theme. Washington and Peking had, he claimed, an identity of views on global strategic matters: 'In Southeast Asia we share the common objective of reducing and eliminating the Soviet presence, bringing about a Vietnamese withdrawal from Kampuchea, and possibly from Laos, and the emergence of a neutral and non-aligned Laos and Kampuchea so as to provide a buffer between Vietnam and Asean.'[44] Nayan Chanda commented at this time that US officials generally seemed sympathetic to the Chinese strategy of isolating and weakening Vietnam by economic, diplomatic and military means. With greater accuracy he might have recognized that it was the Chinese who had accepted the American strategy against Vietnam – one that had been pursued in various forms since 1950.

Summarizing the succession of events since 1975 one reporter has stated:

> Vietnam, at that time, was looking to the United States and the West for help in rebuilding its war-torn country; but when this was repeatedly blocked, it looked increasingly to the Soviets. This, in turn, exacerbated Chinese paranoia about Vietnam becoming a Soviet client. China, in turn, increased its support for Pol Pot in his war with Hanoi and also increased its own pressure on Vietnam. So, a chain of events began, which eventually culminated in the multiple crises and tragedies of 1979.[45]

As we have seen, the outcome of those crises was, for Vietnam, international ostracism and economic chaos. By the end of 1980, there were few indications that the Vietnamese would be able to overcome their problems, at least not in the immediate future. The view of one sympathetic but pessimistic commentator was that 'on all levels, economic, political and ideological, the influence of Western Europe and the US is clearly in the ascendant in South East Asia and ... this is likely to continue through the 1980s with adverse consequences for the domestic needs of the people and the movements for national independence and socialism in the region'.[46] On the other hand, Nguyen Khac Vien, Director of the official Hanoi publication *Vietnamese Studies*, takes a stance in which realism is leavened with optimism: 'We will have some very hard years ahead. In home affairs our country is confronting quite new problems, very hard ones. In foreign affairs we have to confront powerful enemies.... False moves and temporary setbacks are inevitable, but we believe that we will eventually achieve our aims: to keep our national independence, build socialism, and have friendly, peaceful co-operation with other peoples.'[47]

Time will tell which prediction was the more realistic.

DIENBIENPHU

Dienbienphu was situated near the border with Laos in a large valley which produced some 2,000 tons of rice per year and was an important centre for the processing of opium, a commodity traded on the black market by the Vietminh in exchange for US weapons and medical supplies. At the junction of a road network, it was, according to Giap, a 'strategic position of first importance, capable of becoming an infantry and air base of extreme efficiency'.

The French had lost control of Dienbienphu at the end of November 1952. On 2 November 1953 General Navarre, the French commander-in-chief, ordered its reoccupation by a date not later than 1 December. General Cogny, designated commander of the operation, felt it was misconceived but was later reconciled to attempting to use Dienbienphu as a 'mooring point' for guerrilla warfare against the Vietminh. While Cogny feared that Dienbienphu would become a 'battalion meat-grinder', Colonel Nicot, the officer commanding air transport, warned Navarre that it would be impossible to maintain a constant flow of supplies to the valley which, although it possessed a small Japanese-built airstrip, was 200 miles distant from the main French base at Hanoi. Nevertheless, on 20 November, Operation Castor was launched and within a few days French paratroops had dislodged the enemy and secured the position.

Giap decided to 'wipe out at all costs' the whole enemy force at Dienbienphu. As he began to concentrate his divisions it became clear that the 'mooring point' concept would have to be abandoned. On 3 December Navarre ordered his troops to prepare for a pitched defensive battle, believing that their superior discipline and firepower would overwhelm the enemy and thus tilt the military balance throughout the country in favour of the French. The Vietminh accepted his challenge and made elaborate counter-moves. Rejecting the notion of a rapidly mounted assault before the French were fully prepared, Giap opted for a policy of attrition. In addition, he carried out a number of diversionary operations to disperse the enemy's reserves.

During the next three months the Vietminh performed a remarkable logistical feat. Hundreds of thousands of porters, using reinforced bicycles to carry loads of 450 lb, supplied Giap's soldiers with food, guns and ammunition from China. Guns were dragged inch by inch at night into emplacements tunnelled out of the hills surrounding the valley, enabling their crews to fire straight down at the French positions, including the airstrip. Anti-aircraft guns were also cunningly sited and used to devastating effect. In addition, an elaborate system of trenches, dug at great speed, brought the Vietminh to within a few yards of the French outposts; the endless noise of their digging helped to demoralize the enemy.

On 13 March 1954 Giap launched his offensive. As his barrage smashed the enemy strongpoints Colonel Piroth, the French artillery commander, realizing how tragically he had under-estimated the Vietminh firepower, committed suicide with a hand grenade. For fifty-six days and nights the French resisted heroic-ally in abominable conditions. Exceptionally heavy rains in April swamped their positions, they were short of ammunition and, in the last weeks of the battle, many were fighting on half rations. Even so they inflicted heavy casualties and Giap was obliged to make a special effort to maintain the morale of his own men.

However, by 6 May the French were confined to a space the size of two football pitches when Giap deployed his Russian Katyusha rockets to strike the final blows. On 7 May the French command post was overrun and the garrison was forced to surrender. One day after the loss of Dienbienphu the French delegation at the Geneva Conference sued for peace in Indochina.

Bibliographical note
The bare outline offered here can best be supplemented by reading B. Fall, *Hell in a Very Small Place* (Pall Mall Press, 1967). For an interesting account of the part played by Giap, see R. J. O'Neill, *General Giap: Politician and Strategist* (Cassell Australia, 1969).

REFERENCES

CHAPTER ONE

1. R. Smith, *Viet-Nam and the West*, p. 4.
2. Quoted in S. E. Ambrose, *Rise to Globalism*, p. 322.
3. F. Fitzgerald, *Fire in the Lake*, p. 9.
4. See J. Buttinger, *Vietnam: A Political History*, p. 162; D. G. E. Hall, *A History of South-East Asia*, p. 786.
5. Hall, op. cit., pp. 789–90.
6. Ibid., pp. 786–8; M. E. Gettleman (ed.), *Vietnam, History, Documents, and Opinions on a major world crisis*, p. 30.
7. Buttinger, op. cit., p. 162.
8. R. Smith, 'The Development of Opposition to French Rule in Southern Vietnam 1880–1940', *Past & Present* No. 54, February 1972, p. 94.
9. See M. Osborne, *Region of Revolt: Focus on Southeast Asia*, pp. 41–5.
10. See Buttinger, op. cit., pp. 155–60.
11. In the words of Lord Curzon, their victories 'reverberated through the whispering galleries of the East'.
12. That is, unpaid labour demanded of a tenant by his landlord – a relic of a feudal system.
13. Buttinger, op. cit., p. 158.
14. For a useful biography, see J. Lacouture, *Ho Chi Minh*.
15. Lacouture, op. cit., p. 31.
16. Ibid., p. 32.
17. Ibid.
18. For its programme, see Gettleman, op. cit., pp. 39–41.
19. Buttinger, op. cit., p. 180.
20. Ibid., pp. 175–7.
21. See Smith, *Past & Present* No. 54, p. 129.
22. Osborne, op. cit., p. 63.
23. See B. Fall's comment on his 'hammering away at concrete problems, never bothering with doctrine.', quoted in D. Landau, *Kissinger: The Uses of Power*, p. 161.

CHAPTER TWO

1. Signed in August 1939, it was a non-aggression pact between Germany and the Soviet Union. The Indo-chinese Communist Party, like other communist parties throughout the world, was expected to follow Stalin's line. Hence they could not attack Japan, which was an ally of Nazi Germany.
2. J. Woddis (ed.), *Ho Chi Minh, Selected Articles and Speeches 1920–67*, p. 30.
3. Lacouture, op. cit., p. 68.

4. Smith, *Viet-Nam and the West*, p. 110.
5. See Osborne, op. cit., pp. 58–9.
6. Ian McDonald, 'Ho Chi Minh praised by US intelligence in 1945 as non-communist patriot', *The Times*, 26 February 1973.
7. Ibid.
8. Lacouture, op. cit., pp. 97–8.
9. Gettleman, op. cit., pp. 63–6.
10. Quoted in Lacouture, op. cit., p. 92.
11. Quoted in A. M. Schlesinger Jr., *The Bitter Heritage, Vietnam and American Democracy 1941–66*, p. 11.
12. Ibid., pp. 11–12.
13. G. Rosie, *The British in Vietnam*, p. 51.
14. Ibid., pp. 62–3.
15. Quoted in E. Snow, *The Other Side of the River*, p. 686.
16. Rosie, op. cit., p. 96.
17. Ibid., p. 105.
18. See *Keesings Contemporary Archives*, Vol. VI, p. 7779.
19. Rosie, op. cit., p. 140.
20. D. Lancaster, *The Emancipation of French Indo-China*, p. 127.
21. E. J. Hammer, *The Struggle for Indochina*, pp. 145–6.
22. Quoted in Lacouture, op. cit., p. 104.
23. Quoted in Gettleman, op. cit., p. 70.
24. See Lacouture, op. cit., p. 119.
25. Admiral Thierry d'Argenlieu was French High Commissioner in Indochina.
26. Lacouture, op. cit., p. 149.
27. A. Werth, *France 1940–55*, p. 346.
28. Ibid., p. 447.
29. N. Sheehan *et al.*, *The Pentagon Papers*, p. 9.
30. Ibid.
31. Ibid., pp. 9–10.
32. Gettleman, op. cit., p. 85.
33. B. Fall, *The Two Viet-Nams*, p. 113.
34. For a comprehensive account see J. Roy, *The Battle of Dienbienphu*.
35. See Gettleman, op. cit., p. 119.
36. Sheehan, op. cit., p. 40.
37. Ibid.

CHAPTER THREE

1. See Osborne, op. cit., ch. 6 *Malaya and the Philippines: Two Revolts that Failed*.
2. Ibid., p. 110.
3. Gettleman, op. cit., p. 161.
4. Lacouture, op. cit., p. 168 fn. 2.
5. Fitzgerald, op. cit., p. 69.
6. Lacouture, op. cit., p. 168.
7. Woddis, op. cit., p. 90.
8. D. Eisenhower, *Mandate for Change*, p. 372.
9. See Sheehan, op. cit., pp. 15–19; ibid., pp. 53ff.
10. Ibid., p. 14.
11. For comment on the Truman Doctrine, see H. Higgins, *The Cold War*, pp. 43–6.
12. Gettleman, op. cit., p. 215.
13. Sheehan, op. cit., pp. 19ff.

14. See R. Scheer, *The Genesis of United States Support for Ngo Dinh Diem*, in Gettleman, op. cit., pp. 246–64.
15. D. Warner, *The Last Confucian*, p. 196.
16. See B. S. N. Murti, *Vietnam Divided*, pp. 157–9.
17. See R. Scigliano, *South Vietnam: Nation Under Stress*, pp. 133–4.
18. See N. Chomsky, *The Backroom Boys*, p. 112.
19. Fitzgerald, op. cit., p. 85.
20. Sheehan, op. cit., p. 21.
21. Ibid., pp. 23–4.
22. US State Department, *A Threat to Peace*, pp. 5–7.
23. Sheehan, op. cit., pp. 70–2.
24. M. Taylor, 'South Vietnam: Lavish aid limited progress, Pacific Affairs 1961', quoted in R. Murray (ed.), *Vietnam*, pp. 54–5.
25. F. Greene, *The Enemy*, p. 112.
26. Ibid., p. 113.
27. Gettleman, op. cit., p. 238.
28. Fitzgerald, op. cit., p. 90.
29. See P. Devillers, 'Mistakes of the Diem Government', *China Quarterly*, January–March 1962.
30. Sheehan, op. cit., p. 72.
31. Fitzgerald, op. cit., p. 95.
32. Ibid., pp. 126–7.
33. Ibid.
34. See *Keesings Research Report, South Vietnam, A Political History 1954–70*, pp. 28–9.
35. Such was the view taken in the State Department paper 'A Threat to Peace'.

CHAPTER FOUR

1. T. Draper, *Abuse of Power, U.S. Foreign Policy from Cuba to Vietnam*, p. 44.
2. B. Fall, quoted in N. Chomsky, *At War with Asia*, p. 220.
3. See Chomsky, *The Backroom Boys*, n. 30 pp. 175–6; also, Chomsky, *At War with Asia*, p. 219 and n. 9 pp. 278–9.
4. *Keesings Contemporary Archives*, Vol. XI, p. 15349B.
5. Fitzgerald, op. cit., pp. 223–4.
6. Chomsky, *At War with Asia*, p. 219.
7. Fall, *The Two Viet-Nams*, pp. 160–1.
8. Buttinger, op. cit., pp. 423–4.
9. Gettleman, op. cit., p. 230.
10. Ibid., p. 231.
11. Ibid., p. 230 n. 8.
12. W. Burchett, *Vietnam: Inside Story of the Guerilla War*, pp. 112–14.
13. Lacouture, op. cit., pp. 240–1; Chomsky, *The Backroom Boys*, pp. 127–8.
14. Gettleman, op. cit., pp. 236–7.
15. Ibid., p. 239; Lacouture, 'Le Monde', 15 April 1965, quoted in Murray, *Vietnam*, pp. 121–2; Lacouture, op. cit., p. 241; Draper, op. cit., p. 52.
16. Gettleman, op. cit., p. 239.
17. N. Chomsky, *American Power and the New Mandarins*, p. 233 n. 75; Smith, *Viet-Nam and the West*, pp. 165–6.
18. Chomsky, *American Power and the New Mandarins*, p. 195, pp. 225–6.
19. Fitzgerald, op. cit., p. 148.
20. Sheehan, op. cit., p. 69.
21. For agrovilles, see below, pp. 50–1.

22. D. Halberstam, *The Making of a Quagmire*, p. 63. But see also Chomsky, *The Backroom Boys*, p. 127, where he quotes a use of 'Viet Cong' from May 1959.
23. Buttinger, op. cit., p. 459.
24. For the Front's programme, see Gettleman, op. cit., pp. 265–9.
25. See above, pp. 37–8.
26. Buttinger, op. cit., pp. 434–7.
27. Fitzgerald, op. cit., pp. 148–9.
28. Sheehan, op. cit., p. 86.

CHAPTER FIVE

1. Chomsky, *The Backroom Boys*, p. 125.
2. Sheehan, op. cit., pp. 79 and 82.
3. D. Halberstam, *The Best and the Brightest*, pp. 122–4.
4. Sheehan, op. cit., p. 142.
5. Draper, op. cit., p. 58.
6. See Chomsky, *The Backroom Boys*, p. 9, n. 4 pp. 178–9.
7. See above, p. 30.
8. Sheehan, op. cit., p. 79.
9. Halberstam, *The Best and the Brightest*, p. 299.
10. Ibid., pp. 209–11.
11. Homer Bigart, quoted in Halberstam, *The Making of a Quagmire*, p. 75.
12. See above, pp. 26–7.
13. Quoted in Chomsky, *The Backroom Boys*, p. 8.
14. Halberstam, *The Making of a Quagmire*, p. 186.
15. Chomsky, *The Backroom Boys*, p. 9.
16. Fitzgerald, op. cit., pp. 10–11.
17. Hilsman, quoted in Chomsky, *The Backroom Boys*, p. 8; see also Chomsky, *American Power and the New Mandarins*, p. 205.
18. Sheehan, op. cit., p. 155.
19. Fitzgerald, op. cit., p. 125.
20. Halberstam, *The Best and the Brightest*, p. 186.
21. Ibid., p. 249.
22. Halberstam, *The Making of a Quagmire*, p. 202.
23. Ibid., p. 211.
24. Buttinger, op. cit., p. 466.
25. Halberstam, *The Making of a Quagmire*, p. 199.
26. See Halberstam, *The Best and the Brightest*, pp. 259–62.
27. Sheehan, op. cit., p. 167.
28. Ibid.
29. Ibid., p. 166.
30. Ibid., pp. 194–5.
31. Ibid., p. 197.
32. Ibid., p. 173.
33. Halberstam, *The Best and the Brightest*, p. 265.
34. Sheehan, op. cit., p. 174.
35. A. M. Schlesinger Jr., *A Thousand Days*, p. 845; Halberstam, *The Best and the Brightest*, p. 272.
36. Sheehan, op. cit., p. 178.
37. Ibid., pp. 230–1.

CHAPTER SIX

1. Halberstam, *The Best and the Brightest*, p. 298.
2. Sheehan, op. cit., p. 233.
3. Ibid., pp. 271ff.
4. Ibid., p. 276.
5. Ibid., p. 241.
6. Ibid., p. 233.
7. Quoted in Murray, *Vietnam*, p. 111.
8. Chomsky, *The Backroom Boys*, p. 133.
9. Draper, op. cit., p. 96.
10. For his reply see Gettleman, op. cit., pp. 335–41.
11. See comments on *The Mysterious 325th* in Draper, op. cit., pp. 77–86.
12. Chomsky, *The Backroom Boys*, pp. 130–1.
13. Halberstam, *The Best and the Brightest*, p. 404.
14. Sheehan, op. cit., p. 278.
15. Ibid.
16. See comment by Chomsky, *American Power and the New Mandarins*, pp. 209–10; for further information on McNamara's report see Halberstam, *The Best and the Brightest*, pp. 353–5.
17. Sheehan, op. cit., pp. 247–9.
18. See below p. 65.
19. Sheehan, op. cit., p. 256.
20. Ibid., p. 258.
21. See ibid., pp. 258ff.; Halberstam, *The Best and the Brightest*, pp. 411ff.
22. Sheehan, op. cit., pp. 264–5.
23. Halberstam, *The Best and the Brightest*, p. 417.
24. W. Warbey, *Ho Chi Minh*, p. 172.
25. Halberstam, *The Best and the Brightest*, p. 414.
26. Ibid., pp. 411–12.
27. Sheehan, op. cit., p. 265.
28. Warbey, op. cit., p. 172.
29. In his customary down-to-earth language, Johnson gloated to journalists on 5 August: 'I didn't just screw Ho Chi Minh. I cut his pecker off.' Halberstam, *The Best and the Brightest*, p. 414.
30. Sheehan, op. cit., p. 311.
31. Ibid., pp. 315, 360.
32. Ibid., p. 320.
33. Ibid., p. 336.
34. Ibid., p. 338.
35. Ibid., p. 343.
36. J. Cameron, *Witness*, p. 66.
37. Ibid., p. 67.
38. Chomsky, *American Power and the New Mandarins*, p. 184.
39. Chomsky, *At War with Asia*, p. 227.
40. Sheehan, op. cit., p. 386.
41. Halberstam, *The Best and the Brightest*, p. 599.
42. Sheehan, op. cit., p. 416.
43. Ibid., p. 467.
44. Halberstam, *The Best and the Brightest*, p. 618.
45. Chomsky, *The Backroom Boys*, pp. 98–9; Halberstam, *The Best and the Brightest*, p. 652.
46. Chomsky, *The Backroom Boys*, p. 99.
47. Sheehan, op. cit., p. 592.

48. Ibid., p. 601; Halberstam, *The Best and the Brightest*, p. 653.
49. Sheehan, op. cit., p. 611.

CHAPTER SEVEN

1. Gettleman, op. cit., pp. 341ff. For a less altruistic version of US motives, see McNaughton's memorandum in Sheehan, op. cit., p. 255. See also Chomsky, *For Reasons of State*, p. 235.
2. Paul Johnson, 'America's Suez?', *New Statesman*, 9 February 1968.
3. Chomsky, *The Backroom Boys*, p. 93.
4. Ibid., p. 85.
5. US pilots were involved before 1965; see Chomsky, *The Backroom Boys*, p. 9.
6. Chomsky, *The Backroom Boys*, p. 93.
7. See F. Harvey, *Air War – Vietnam*, ch. 15.
8. Chomsky, *The Backroom Boys*, p. 25.
9. R. A. Falk, G. Kolko, R. J. Lifton (eds.), *Crimes of War*, pp. 411–12.
10. Ibid., p. 411.
11. Ibid., p. 412.
12. Ibid., p. 413.
13. Chomsky, *For Reasons of State*, p. 226; Chomsky, *At War with Asia*, p. 74.
14. Chomsky, *For Reasons of State*, pp. 225–6.
15. See above p. 59.
16. Falk *et al.*, op. cit., p. 288.
17. Ibid., p. 286.
18. Ibid., p. 285.
19. Chomsky, *American Power and the New Mandarins*, p. 254 n. 2.
20. Ibid., p. 255.
21. Falk *et al.*, op. cit., pp. 278–9.
22. Ibid., p. 279.
23. Ibid., pp. 332–3.
24. Ibid., p. 358.
25. Chomsky, *For Reasons of State*, p. 223.
26. Ibid., p. 225.
27. Ibid., pp. 235–6.
28. See R. Hammer, *One Morning in the War, The Tragedy at Pinkville*, p. 197.
29. M. McCarthy, *Vietnam*, p. 55.
30. Buttinger, op. cit., p. 492.
31. Halbertsam, *The Best and the Brightest*, p. 483.
32. For numerous examples see passim W. J. Lederer, *The Anguished American*.
33. Fitzgerald, op. cit., pp. 311–12.
34. Lederer, op. cit., p. 39.
35. Chomsky, *At War with Asia*, pp. 52–3.
36. Chomsky, *The Backroom Boys*, p. 151.
37. Lodge, for example, regarded the Buddhists 'as equivalent to card-carrying Communists.' Chomsky, *The Backroom Boys*, p. 118.
38. Chomsky, *American Power and the New Mandarins*, p. 108 n. 25.
39. Fitzgerald, op. cit., p. 252.
39. Ibid., pp. 349–50.
41. Chomsky, *American Power and the New Mandarins*, pp. 38–9; Draper, op. cit., p. 103.
42. Fitzgerald, op. cit., p. 139.

43. Ibid., p. 195.
44. Ibid., p. 169.
45. Draper, op. cit., p. 97.
46. Buttinger, op. cit., p. 487.
47. Chomsky, *The Backroom Boys*, p. 82.
48. Ibid.
49. Sheehan, op. cit., pp. 550–1; Halberstam, *The Best and the Brightest*, p. 643.
50. Simon Winchester, 'LBJ sanctioned secret bombing', *The Guardian*, 10 August 1973.

CHAPTER EIGHT

1. Halberstam, *The Best and the Brightest*, p. 512.
2. Ibid., p. 530.
3. See Draper, op. cit., pp. 16–21.
4. C. Reich, *The Greening of America*, p. 194.
5. Quoted in Snow, op. cit., p. 709.
6. Quoted in J. Bosch, *Pentagonism, A Substitute for Imperialism*, p. 9.
7. Ibid., p. 10.
8. Ibid., p. 115.
9. Halberstam, *The Best and the Brightest*, p. 645.
10. Buttinger, op. cit., pp. 489–90.
11. See J. J. Zasloff & A. E. Goodman (eds.), *Indochina in Conflict, A Political Assessment*, p. 205.
12. Bosch, op. cit., p. 37.
13. For a comment on élites see Chomsky, *At War with Asia*, p. 26.
14. Buttinger, op. cit., p. 490.
15. Fitzgerald, op. cit., p. 303.
16. Halberstam, *The Best and the Brightest*, p. 609.
17. Buttinger, op. cit., p. 490.
18. Ibid., p. 491.
19. Ibid., pp. 490–1.
20. R. Segal, *America's Receding Future*, p. 250.
21. Ibid., pp. 260–1.
22. See N. Mailer, *The Armies of the Night*, pp. 296–7.
23. Chomsky, *American Power and the New Mandarins*, p. 316.
24. Schlesinger, *The Bitter Heritage*, p. 121.
25. Ibid., p. 49.
26. Ibid., p. 144.
27. Ibid., p. 52.
28. Chomsky, *At Wat with Asia*, pp. 62–3.
29. Chomsky, *The Backroom Boys*, p. 78.
30. Chomsky, *American Power and the New Mandarins*, p. 12.
31. Bosch, op. cit., p. 12.
32. Ibid., p. 85.
33. Ibid., p. 68.
34. Ibid., p. 5.
35. Halberstam, *The Best and the Brightest*, p. 640.
36. Fitzgerald, op. cit., p. 394.
37. Halberstam, *The Best and the Brightest*, p. 648.
38. Ibid., p. 662.

CHAPTER NINE

1. Fitzgerald, op. cit., p. 403.
2. Ibid., p. 468 n. 15.
3. Don Oberdorfer, quoted in D. Halberstam, 'The Reign of Lyndon B. Nixonger', *New Statesman*, 19 May 1972.
4. See L. Heren, *No Hail, No Farewell*, p. 226.
5. Fitzgerald, op. cit., p. 406 n. 2.
6. Ibid., pp. 406–7.
7. Ibid., p. 405.
8. Ibid., p. 407.
9. Quoted in R. West, 'Vietnam: The Year of the Rat', *New Statesman*, 25 February 1972.
10. Chomsky, *The Backroom Boys*, pp. 199–200.
11. Ibid., p. 104.
12. Fitzgerald, op. cit., p. 418.
13. Chomsky, *At War with Asia*, p. 116.
14. N. Sihanouk & W. Burchett, *My War With the CIA*, p. 52.
15. Leading article, 'Mr. Nixon's private wars', *The Guardian*, 6 August 1973.
16. Sihanouk & Burchett, op. cit., p. 59.
17. Ibid., p. 259.
18. Ibid., pp. 170–1
19. Chomsky, *At War with Asia*, p. 179.
20. Ibid., p. 273.
21. Sheehan, op. cit., p. 239.
22. Simon Winchester, 'LBJ sanctioned secret bombing', *The Guardian*, 10 August 1973.
23. Leading article, 'Mr. Nixon's private wars', *The Guardian*, 6 August 1973; article, 'Nixon "lied" over raids into Laos', *The Guardian*, 13 August 1973.
24. Peter Dale Scott, 'Laos: The Story Nixon Won't Tell', *New York Review of Books*, 9 April 1970, p. 39. Scott quotes another source suggesting that 20,000 sorties were being flown per month, see n. 28.
25. Chomsky, *At War with Asia*, p. 195.
26. Ibid.
27. Chomsky, *The Backroom Boys*, p. 37.
28. See H. Arendt, *Crises of the Republic*, pp. 9ff.
29. See Halberstam, *The Best and the Brightest*, pp. 409–10.
30. See R. Hammer, *One Morning in the War*.
31. Chomsky, *At War with Asia*, p. 81.
32. Fitzgerald, op. cit., p. 377.
33. R. Hammer, op. cit., p. 175.
34. Ibid., pp. 197ff.
35. Falk *et al.*, op. cit., p. 466.
36. Chomsky, *For Reasons of State*, p. 224.
37. Falk *et al.*, op. cit., pp. 466–7.
38. Chomsky, *At War with Asia*, pp. 232–3.
39. Chomsky, *American Power and the New Mandarins*, p. 224; Chomsky, *The Backroom Boys*, p. 129; Falk *et al.*, op. cit., p. 265.
40. Chomsky, *At War with Asia*, p. 234.
41. R. West, 'Vietnam: The Year of the Rat', *New Statesman*, 25 February 1972.
42. J. Fox, 'Vietnamisation: The price they had to pay', *Sunday Times Magazine*, 25 June 1972.
43. Article, 'The failure of American bombing', *Sunday Times*, 7 May 1972.
44. Gavin Young, 'Now that the GIs have gone', *Observer*, 1 April 1973.
45. R. West, *Vietnam: The Year of the Rat*.

46. Zasloff & Goodman, op. cit., p. 219.
47. J. Fox, *Vietnamisation: The price they had to pay.*
48. Ibid.
49. R. Littauer, 'Twenty million dollars of death a day', *The Times*, 26 May 1972.
50. Anthony Lewis, 'What they talk about when B52s pound Hanoi', *Observer*, 18 June 1972.
51. Marc Ribou & Sven Oste, 'Giant-Killers', *Observer Magazine*, 17 December 1972.
52. Ibid.
53. Anthony Lewis, 'Widening cracks in Dr. Kissinger's facade', *The Times*, 20 December 1972. See also a pamphlet, *The British Press and Vietnam*, published by the Indochina Solidarity conference.
54. Alex Finer, 'Why B52s are in trouble', *Sunday Times*, 24 December 1972.
55. Jean Leclerc du Sablon & Jean Thoraval, 'Hanoi survives in its "caves"', *Sunday Times*, 31 December 1972.
56. Letter in *The Times*, 30 December 1972.
57. Michael Allen, 'How it feels to be bombed in Hanoi', *Sunday Times*, 31 December 1972.
58. Alex Finer, *Why B52s are in trouble.*
59. See Chomsky, *The Backroom Boys*, p. 160.

CHAPTER TEN

1. J. Buttinger, *Vietnam – The Unforgettable Tragedy*, p. 124.
2. Ibid., p. 129.
3. Ibid., p. 127.
4. Murray Sayle, 'Lyrical words from Paris sound like a sick joke in Saigon', *Sunday Times*, 28 January 1973.
5. Buttinger, *Vietnam – The Unforgettable Tragedy*, p. 134.
6. Ibid., p. 135.
7. G. Porter, *A Peace Denied*, p. 264.
8. Ibid., p. 268.
9. Van Tien Dung, *Our Great Spring Victory*, p. 13.
10. Ibid., pp. 99–100.
11. Buttinger, *Vietnam – The Unforgettable Tragedy*, p. 149.
12. Ibid., p. 151.
13. W. Burchett, *Catapult to Freedom*, p. 43.
14. Van Tien Dung, op. cit., p. 274.
15. Buttinger, *Vietnam – The Unforgettable Tragedy*, pp. 94–5.
16. Burchett, *Catapult to Freedom*, p. 4.
17. Ibid., pp. 45–6.
18. Phan Huy Le et al. (eds), *Our Military Traditions.*
19. E. Martin, *Reaching the Other Side*, p. 219.
20. A. Barnett, 'Inter-Communist Conflicts and Vietnam', *Marxism Today*, August 1979, p. 245.
21. W. Burchett, *Grasshoppers and Elephants*, p. 255.
22. G. Lewy, *America in Vietnam*, p. 427.
23. Buttinger, *Vietnam – The Unforgettable Tragedy*, p. 169.
24. Ibid., p. 178.
25. N. Chomsky & E. S. Herman, *After the Cataclysm*, p. 14.
26. Lewy, op. cit., p. 441.
27. Chomsky & Herman, op. cit., p. 21.

CHAPTER ELEVEN

1. Chomsky & Herman, op. cit., p. 10.
2. *US Chemical Warfare and its Consequences*, p. 103.
3. Ibid., p. 13.
4. Ibid., p. 19.
5. Burchett, *Grasshoppers and Elephants*, p. 213.
6. Porter, op. cit., p. 272.
7. *Far Eastern Economic Review*, 16 May 1975, p. 10.
8. *With Firm Steps*, pp. 80 ff.
9. Ibid., pp. 81–2.
10. *Far Eastern Economic Review*, 11 June 1976, p. 32.
11. F. Snepp, *Decent Interval*, p. 567.
12. Chomsky & Herman, op. cit., pp. 61–2.
13. *Far Eastern Economic Review*, 23 May 1975, p. 13.
14. Ibid., 6 June 1975, p. 10.
15. Buttinger, *Vietnam – The Unforgettable Tragedy*, p. 157.
16. K. Gough, *Ten Times More Beautiful*, p. 256.
17. *Far Eastern Economic Review*, 23 May 1975, p. 13.
18. Ibid., 11 June 1976, p. 32.
19. Martin, op. cit., p. 275.
20. Burchett, *Grasshoppers and Elephants*, p. 245.
21. Ibid., p. 209; Chomsky & Herman, op. cit., pp. 68–9.
22. Burchett, *Grasshoppers and Elephants*, pp. 207 ff.
23. *Far Eastern Economic Review*, 13 May 1977, p. 42.
24. Ibid., 23 September 1977, p. 31.

CHAPTER TWELVE

1. Gough, op. cit., p. 238.
2. *Far Eastern Economic Review*, 20 May 1977, p. 16.
3. Porter, op. cit., p. 325.
4. *Vietnam South East Asia International*, April–June 1980, p. 2.
5. Chomsky & Herman, op. cit., p. 320 n. 22.
6. *Vietnam South East Asia International*, April–June 1980, p. 19.
7. *Far Eastern Economic Review*, 3 October 1980, p. 15.
8. Ibid., 4 May 1979, pp. 8–9.
9. Ibid., 22 December 1978, p. 8.
10. For a full treatment of events in Cambodia see Chomsky & Herman, op. cit., Ch. 6.
11. *Far Eastern Economic Review*, 2 February 1979, p. 18.
12. Ibid., 21 April 1978, p. 22.
13. Ibid., 19 January 1979, p. 13.
14. Barnett, op. cit., pp. 18 ff.
15. Nguyen Khac Vien, *Vietnam '80*, pp. 40 ff.
16. *Far Eastern Economic Review*, 9 June 1978, p. 11.
17. Ibid., 19 January 1979, pp. 12–14.
18. Ibid., 5 January 1979, p. 9.
19. *The Guardian*, 2 July 1979, quoted in *Keesing's*, Vol. XXVI, pp. 30075–6.
20. *Financial Times*, 4 August 1978, quoted in *Keesing's*, Vol. XXV. p. 29469.
21. *Far Eastern Economic Review*, 20 October 1978, pp. 13–14.
22. Ibid., 27 July 1979, pp. 19–20.
23. Ibid., 22 June 1979, p. 17.

24. Ibid., 29 June 1979, p. 10.
25. Ibid., 27 July 1979, p. 19.
26. Ibid., 24 August 1979, p. 18.
27. Chomsky & Herman, op. cit., pp. 56–7.
28. *The Guardian*, 17 July 1979, quoted in *Keesing's*, Vol. XXVI, p. 30075.
29. *Vietnam South East Asia International*, January–March 1979, p. 4.
30. *Far Eastern Economic Review*, 23 March 1979, p. 9.
31. Ibid., 4 August 1978, p. 13.
32. Ibid., 29 February 1980, p. 14.
33. Ibid., 26 September 1980, p. 23.
34. Ibid.
35. Ibid., 9 January 1981, p. 40.
36. Ibid., p. 42.
37. Ibid., 1 August 1980, pp. 37 ff.
38. Ibid., 27 February 1980, pp. 38 ff.
39. Ibid., 9 January 1981, pp. 42 ff.
40. Ibid., 27 February 1981, pp. 32–3.
41. Ibid., pp. 31–2.
42. Ibid., p. 30.
43. Ibid., 25 January 1980, p. 17.
44. Ibid., 3 October 1980, p. 15. The 'identity of views between Washington and Peking was reflected in the informal truce in Kampuchea between the Khmer Rouge, supported by China, and the Western-backed Khmer Serei: see *Kessing's*, Vol. XXVII, p. 30669. The Vietnamese were in Laos with the agreement of the Laotian government. Details of the treaty of friendship and co-operation between Laos and Vietnam, signed on 18 July 1977, are given in *Keesing's*, Vol. XXIV, pp. 28765 ff. On Laos see also Chomsky & Herman, op. cit., Ch. 5.
45. *Vietnam South East Asia International*, April–June 1980, p. 2.
46. Ibid., p. 20.
47. Nguyen Khac Vien, *Vietnam '80*, p. 66.

BIBLIOGRAPHY

Ambrose, S. E., *Rise to Globalism* (Allen Lane, 1971)
Arendt, H., *Crises of the Republic* (Penguin, 1973)

Bator, V., *Vietnam, A Diplomatic Tragedy: Origins of U.S. Involvement* (Faber & Faber, 1967)
Bosch, J., *Pentagonism, a substitute for imperialism* (Grove Press, 1968)
Burchett, W., *Vietnam: Inside Story of the Guerrilla War* (International Publishers, 1954)
Burchett, W., *Grasshoppers and Elephants* (Urizen Books, 1977)
  Catapult to Freedom (Quartet Books, 1978)
Buttinger, J., *Vietnam: A Political History* (André Deutsch, 1969)
Buttinger, J., *Vietnam – The Unforgettable Tragedy* (André Deutsch, 1977)

Cameron, J., *Witness* (V. Gollancz, 1966)
Chomsky, N., *American Power and the New Mandarins* (Penguin, 1969)

At War with Asia (Fontana/Collins, 1971)
  The Backroom Boys (Fontana/Collins, 1973)
  For Reasons of State (Fontana/Collins, 1973)
Chomsky, N. & Herman, E. S., *After the Cataclysm* (Spokesman, 1979)

Dawson, A., *55 Days: The Fall of South Vietnam* (Prentice-Hall, 1977)
Draper, T., *Abuse of Power, U.S. Foreign Policy from Cuba to Vietnam* (Penguin, 1969)

Eisenhower, D. D., *Mandate for Change* (Heinemann, 1963)

Falk, R. A., *Vietnam and International Law* (O'Hare, 1967)
Falk, R. A., Kolko, G., Lifton, R. J. (eds.), *Crimes of War* (Vintage Books, 1971)
Fall, B., *The Two Viet-Nams* (Pall Mall Press, 1965)
  Viet-Nam Witness (Pall Mall Press, 1966)
Far Eastern Economic Review (1975–80)
Fenn, C., *Ho Chi Minh* (Studio Vista, 1973)
Fitzgerald, F., *Fire in the Lake* (Macmillan, 1972)
Fulbright, J. W., *The Arrogance of Power* (Penguin, 1970)

Gelb, L. H. & Betts, R. K., *The Irony of Vietnam* (Brookings Institution, 1979)
Gerassi, J., *North Vietnam: A Documentary* (Allen & Unwin, 1968)
Gettleman, M. E. (ed.), *Vietnam, History, Documents, and Opinions on a Major World Crisis* (Penguin, 1966)
Giap, Vo Nguyen, *Big Victory, Great Task* (Frederick Praeger, 1968)
Gomes, C. M., *The Kampuchea Connection* (Grassroots, 1980)
Gough, K., *Ten Times More Beautiful* (Monthly Review Press, 1978)
Greene, F., *Vietnam! Vietnam!* (J. Cape, 1967)
  The Enemy (J. Cape, 1970)

Halberstam, D., *The Making of a Quagmire* (Bodley Head, 1965)
  The Best and the Brightest (Barrie & Jenkins, 1972)
Hall, D. G. E., *A History of South-East Asia* (Macmillan, 1968)
Hammer, E. J., *The Struggle for Indochina* (Stanford University Press, 1954)
Hammer, R., *One Morning in the War, The Tragedy at Pinkville* (Rupert Hart-Davis, 1970)
Harvey, F., *Air War – Vietnam* (Bantam, 1967)
Heren, L., *No Hail, No Farewell* (Weidenfeld & Nicolson, 1970)
Higgins, H., *The Cold War* (Heinemann Educational Books, 1974)

Indochina Solidarity Conference, *The British Press and Vietnam* (1973)

Keesing's Research Report,
  South Vietnam, A Political History (Scribners, 1970)
Kiernan, V. G., *The Lords of Human Kind* (Penguin, 1972)
Knoebl, K., Victor Charlie, *The Face of War in Vietnam* (Pall Mall Press, 1967)

Lacouture, J., *Ho Chi Minh* (Penguin, 1968)
Lancaster, D., *The Emancipation of French Indo-China* (O.U.P., 1961)

Vietnam

Landau, D., *Kissinger: The Uses of Power* (Robson Books, 1974)
Lederer, W. J., *The Anguished American* (V. Gollancz, 1969)
Lewy, G., *America in Vietnam* (O.U.P., 1978)

McCarthy, M., *Vietnam* (Penguin, 1968)
 Hanoi (Penguin, 1969)
McCarthy, R. D., *The Ultimate Folly* (V. Gollancz, 1970)
Mailer, N., *The Armies of the Night* (Penguin, 1970)
Martin, E. S., *Reaching the Other Side* (Crown Publishers, 1978)
Murray, R. (ed.), *Vietnam* (Eyre & Spottiswoode, 1965)
Murti, B. S. N., *Vietnam Divided* (Asia Publishing House, 1964)

Nguyen Khac Vien, *Vietnam – patrie retrouvée* (Editions sociales, 1977)
Nguyen Khac Vien, *Vietnam '80* (Vietnam Courier, 1980)

O'Neill, R. J., *General Giap: Politician and Strategist* (Cassell, 1969)
Osborne, M., *Region of Revolt: Focus on Southeast Asia* (Penguin, 1971)

Phan Huy Le *et al.* (eds), *Our Military Traditions* (Vietnamese Studies No. 55, Hanoi)
Porter, G., *A Peace Denied* (Indiana University Press, 1975)

Reich, C., *The Greening of America* (Penguin, 1972)
Rosie, G., *The British in Vietnam* (Panther, 1970)
Roy, J., *The Battle of Dienbienphu* (Faber & Faber, 1965)

Salisbury, H., *Behind the Lines – Hanoi* (Secker & Warburg, 1967)
Schlesinger, A. M. Jr., *A Thousand Days* (André Deutsch, 1965)
 The Bitter Heritage, Vietnam and American Democracy 1941–1966 (André Deutsch, 1967)
Scigliano, R., *South Vietnam: Nation Under Stress* (Houghton Mifflin Co., 1963)
Segal, R., *America's Receding Future* (Penguin, 1970)
Sharp, U. S. G., *Strategy for Defeat* (Presidio Press, 1978)
Sheehan, N. *et al.*, *The Pentagon Papers* (Bantam, 1971)
Sihanouk, N. & Burchett, W., *My War With The CIA* (Penguin, 1973)
Smith, R., *Viet-Nam and the West* (Heinemann Educational Books, 1968)
Snepp, F., *Decent Interval* (Random House, 1977)
Snow, E., *The Other Side of the River* (V. Gollancz, 1963)

Terzani, T., *Giai Phong! The Fall and Liberation of Saigon* (Angus & Robertson, 1976)
Thompson, R., *No Exit from Vietnam* (Chatto & Windus, 1969)

US Chemical Warfare and its Consequences (Vietnam Courier, 1980)

Van Tien Dung, *Our Great Spring Victory* (Monthly Review Press, 1977)
Viet Tran, *Vietnam: j'ai choisi l'exil* (Editions du Seuil, 1979)

Warbey, W., *Ho Chi Minh* (Merlin Press, 1972)

Warner, D., *The Last Confucian* (Penguin, 1964)
Werth, A., *France 1940–1955* (Robert Hale, 1956)
With Firm Steps: Southern Vietnam Since Liberation 1975–1977 (Foreign Languages Publishing House, Hanoi, 1978)
Woddis, J., *Ho Chi Minh, Selected Articles and Speeches 1920–1967* (Lawrence & Wishart, 1969)

Zasloff, J. J. & Goodman, A. E., *Indochina in Conflict, A Political Assessment* (D. C. Heath, 1972)

INDEX